T0037623

"*Helping Your Child with Sensory Regulation* is a tremendous resource for parents of children whose nervous systems result in behaviors that may be challenging and exasperating. The authors walk readers through relatable examples of how attempts to self-regulate can lead to behaviors that appear odd, mimic psychiatric disorders, or appear willfully defiant, and they provide accessible and effective solutions. All parents will find useful guidance in this practical book."

—**Britt Rathbone, MSSW, LCSW-C**, adolescent therapist, and coauthor of *Dialectical Behavior Therapy for At-Risk Adolescents*, *What Works with Teens*, and *Parenting a Teen Who Has Intense Emotions*

"This outstanding resource for parents of children with sensory dysregulation represents an extraordinary combination of the authors' extensive knowledge and their ability to present complex issues in easily understandable language. Engaging clinical vignettes and self-awareness exercises facilitate understanding of how sensory dysregulation might be experienced and observed, and evidence-based principles of behavioral treatments drive presentation of practical and helpful coping strategies to improve parent and child satisfaction with life."

—**Melinda A. Stanley, PhD**, distinguished emeritus professor of psychiatry and behavioral sciences at Baylor College of Medicine; and coauthor of a leading textbook, *Abnormal Psychology*

"This book is a gem! At once both comprehensive and practical, it is filled with pearls of wisdom amassed over decades of clinical experience with children and families. Written by two of the field's finest clinicians, it is rooted in the best-available science and crafted in a manner that is accessible and relatable for parents. Mouton-Odum and Goldfinger Golomb understand the parent perspective so well, and they write with compassion while delivering sound, solid advice. I look forward to sharing this resource with my own trainees, colleagues, and patients."

—**Tara S. Peris, PhD**, associate professor of psychiatry and biobehavioral sciences at the UCLA Semel Institute, and program director of the UCLA ABC Partial Hospitalization Program

"Ruth Goldfinger Golomb and Suzanne Mouton-Odum are two of the most experienced and thoughtful therapists in practice. Here, they tear apart the complex emotional and behavioral results of sensory sensitivity, and provide case studies to translate these ideas into real life. Parents seeking help for their child will find practical advice and tools, and the relief of many 'aha' moments of self-recognition. Importantly, they'll also receive the additional, vital gift of workable self-care strategies for themselves."

—**Jennifer Raikes**, executive director of The TLC Foundation for Body-Focused Repetitive Behaviors; and director of *Bad Hair Life*, a documentary about living with trichotillomania

"This book is a breath of fresh air for parents who have been struggling to understand how to help their children who have sensory struggles. Not only have the authors provided easy-to-understand explanations of why your child is struggling, they also give step-by-step and easy-to-follow guidance on how to increase your child's ability to cope and be more functional in the face of their sensory triggers."

—**Litsa Tanner, MS, MFT,** cofounder of the Santa Rosa
Center for Cognitive Behavioral Therapy, and adjunct
faculty member at the University of San Francisco

"This book provides welcome guidance for parents whose children have problems regulating their sensory world. The authors cast a bright light on a poorly understood contributor to common family problems, and to many clinical disorders as well. In plain language, readers are helped to understand the nature of these problems, and to develop a practical and scientifically sound plan for helping children manage their uncooperative sensory systems."

—**Charles S. Mansueto, PhD,** founder and director of
the Behavior Therapy Center of Greater Washington in
Silver Spring, MD—a leading center for the treatment
of obsessive-compulsive and related disorders

Helping Your Child *with* Sensory Regulation

Skills to Manage the Emotional *and* Behavioral Components of Your Child's Sensory Processing Challenges

SUZANNE MOUTON-ODUM, PhD

RUTH GOLDFINGER GOLOMB, LCPC

New Harbinger Publications, Inc.

Publisher's Note

This publication is designed to provide accurate and authoritative information in regard to the subject matter covered. It is sold with the understanding that the publisher is not engaged in rendering psychological, financial, legal, or other professional services. If expert assistance or counseling is needed, the services of a competent professional should be sought.

Distributed in Canada by Raincoast Books

Copyright © 2021 by Suzanne Mouton-Odum and Ruth Goldfinger Golomb
New Harbinger Publications, Inc.
5674 Shattuck Avenue
Oakland, CA 94609
www.newharbinger.com

Sensory Processing Disorder Checklist reproduced from *Psychological Interventions for Children with Sensory Dysregulation* by Ruth Golomb and Suzanne Mouton-Odum. © 2016 by the Guilford Press.

Cover design by Amy Daniel; Acquired by Tesilya Hanauer;
Edited by Jennifer Eastman

All Rights Reserved

Library of Congress Cataloging-in-Publication Data

Names: Mouton-Odum, Suzanne, author. | Golomb, Ruth Goldfinger, author. |
  Penzel, Fred, author.
Title: Helping your child with sensory regulation : skills to manage the emotional and
  behavioral components of your child's sensory processing challenges / by Suzanne
  Mouton-Odum, PhD. and Ruth Golomb, Fred Penzel, LCPC.
Description: Oakland, CA : New Harbinger Publications, [2021] | Includes bibliograph-
  ical references.
Identifiers: LCCN 2020040278 (print) | LCCN 2020040279 (ebook) | ISBN
  9781684036264 (trade paperback) | ISBN 9781684036271 (pdf) | ISBN
  9781684036288 (epub)
Subjects: LCSH: Sensory integration dysfunction in children. | Sensory disorders in
  children--Treatment.
Classification: LCC RJ496.S44 M68 2021 (print) | LCC RJ496.S44 (ebook) | DDC
  618.92/8--dc23
LC record available at https://lccn.loc.gov/2020040278
LC ebook record available at https://lccn.loc.gov/2020040279

Printed in the United States of America

23   22   21

10   9   8   7   6   5   4   3   2   1   First Printing

This book is dedicated to all of the children and families we have met and worked with who live with sensory regulation issues. You inspire us every day and have helped us develop compassionate, supportive, and creative ways to help you live sensational lives!

Contents

Foreword

As a cognitive behavioral psychologist and the parent of an autistic person, I have long been acquainted with sensory issues in both children and adults. When I first began treating people, nearly forty years ago, we had no real understanding of or names for these problems, nor did we have any evidence-based techniques to use with those who came to us seeking help. Many practitioners with older-type training looked at these individuals and simply assumed their problems were purely psychological and that they could somehow be talked or medicated out of them. Some parents got no better answer than the old "They'll grow out of it." This left the vast majority of these folks with nowhere to turn and with no explanation for what was happening to them.

Since that time, there has been a gradual increase in our knowledge of problems involving the nervous system and how to treat them. This is not to say that our understanding is by any means complete or that newer, more effective treatments have yet to be developed. It almost seems that the more we learn about the brain and the rest of the nervous system, the more we find that we do not know. In the meantime, however, we do seem to be more effective in treating sensory problems and are constantly at work in our attempts to do even better.

The fact that this book has even been written is a good indicator of the progress we have made. I look back on people I encountered in treatment decades ago and dearly wish I had had the level of information presented here so that I could have better helped them. I watched my own son struggle with serious sensory issues and as my wife and I tried to help him cope, we found ourselves without anyone to advise us. It all seemed so mysterious. We basically had to find our own way. Many of the helpful things we originally learned about dealing with sensory issues—and that you will read about in this book—were things we observed firsthand in our own home. This was where I first put together my own theories regarding over- and under-stimulation. We learned there was no single all-encompassing solution. Some of our own son's problems seemed to improve with maturity, some we were able to help him manage with hard work, and some we just learned to live with. Things improved, but it would have been nice to not have to have reinvented the wheel in getting there.

Unfortunately, there are still far too few professionals who have the training and experience to understand how to diagnose and treat sensory difficulties in children and adults. Even in populated areas with many professionals, you may well find yourself on your own and without anyone to help you, just as my wife and I did. That is where a book like this comes in. It not only describes this complex problem in clear terms, but it also gives you a way to create your own program so that you do not have to feel isolated and helpless. It is a true resource, and the next best thing to being able to sit down and consult with Ruth and Suzanne.

I have been personally and professionally acquainted with both the authors of this book for many years, and that I know of few practitioners who are as knowledgeable, dedicated, and professional as they are. Their experience is truly extensive, learned on the job, and the information they share is meaningful and useful. Do they have magical solutions to all sensory problems? No, no one does, but what you will learn from this book is that while there are no quick fixes, there is hope and there are solutions if you are willing to work on them. Left to their own devices, people with sensory issues try to find their own solutions, which, unfortunately, may not work very well, and which often cause them further difficulties. Our job, and theirs, is to continue to seek and learn better, more adaptive ways of dealing with those whose brain functioning can sometimes be extremely confusing and disruptive of their ability to live a normal life. This book will surely be of great help with this task.

—Fred Penzel, PhD

Introduction
What Happens When There Is a Problem with Sensory Regulation?

We each have a unique nervous system, and, consequently, each of us is a little different in terms of how our nervous system experiences the world. For example, I may like a 65-degree temperature in my house, and you might prefer 75 degrees. I may like roller coasters, and you might prefer stillness and quiet. When it comes to the nervous system, there are no "rights" or "wrongs," just differences. Our nervous system helps us notice things that are happening both inside and outside our bodies. It helps us sense heat or cold, see colors and shapes, experience a rapidly beating heart or a sense of calm in our bodies. Our senses make up the nervous system. After decades of working with people in the therapy office, we have observed how the uniqueness of our nervous systems profoundly impacts our beliefs, preferences, choices, behaviors, and even moods.

How does the nervous system affect emotional, behavioral, and psychological functioning? We use our senses to understand the world around us. However, each one of us perceives our world a little differently. This is true whether it is a favorite color, genre of music, or variety of cuisine. Preferences such as these can shape hobbies, relationships, and career choices. For example, a child who has a keen eye for detail might grow up to be an architect, artist, or interior designer. Someone who thrives on movement may become a ballet dancer or work at some other kind of job that does not require hours behind a desk. Conversely, negative or unpleasant sensory experiences can also shape preferences. Someone who cannot stand the look of clutter might prefer minimalist design, and a person who becomes upset around loud noises might choose to work in a library or an art museum.

In more extreme cases, unpleasant sensory experiences can cause anxious feelings or unusual behaviors. For example, if the sensation of wind blowing on your face is extremely uncomfortable, you might refuse to ride in a car with the windows down (let alone in a convertible) or avoid going to the beach on a windy day. These behaviors might be confusing to the people around you. They might wonder why you hate convertibles and beaches, or they might just think that you are being stubborn or rude. Understanding these sensory experiences and the subsequent reactions is the focus of this book. Oftentimes, a child's reaction may seem extreme, which can confuse, frustrate, or even anger other people, and it may interfere with the child's relationships. Extreme reactions can interfere with the child's functioning in the home or classroom. For example, if a child is sensitive to visual stimuli, entering a bright, cluttered room can actually make them feel nervous or uncomfortable, even if they are not quite sure why. This response is no different from that of a child who becomes anxious when they see a clown or are frightened by a large dog. Although the stimulus is different, the sensation of anxiety and the response can be exactly the same.

In addition to sensory "likes" and "dislikes," the nervous system also detects imbalances in the system and seeks to achieve a sense of balance with arousal and calming behaviors. Neither extreme is ideal, so the nervous system seeks balance through different activities that calm the overstimulation and energize the under-stimulation. For example, when an adult is overstimulated (after a very long, stressful day), they might go for a run, take a hot bath, or have a glass of wine to achieve a sense of calm and, in essence, balance. When under-stimulated (after sitting in a long meeting at three in the afternoon), an adult might seek caffeine or a snack, or might take a quick walk to energize the nervous system. People are constantly in the business of keeping their bodies in balance to achieve that sense of equilibrium. We will describe this process in greater detail in the next chapter.

Children are no different in terms of their need to stay in balance, although they have not learned the skills to do so. After an overstimulating day at the amusement park, a child may become irritable or cry easily, even without knowing why. When feeling under-stimulated, the same child may become wiggly, jump up and down, or annoy people around them to seek stimulation. As adults, most of us have learned how to manage our complex nervous systems, but children are still learning these skills. This book will help you recognize and understand what is happening with your child to better understand their nervous system and their behavior.

When seemingly small things create big internal sensations, a sense of discomfort or even panic can follow. This is referred to as "sensory dysregulation." How does it feel to have a dysregulated nervous system? Imagine having the flu and what a relief it is to lie in a soft bed in a quiet, dark room. Now imagine suffering from the flu while lying on an anthill, listening to rock music at high volume, and trying to compute calculus. Every nerve ending in your body is reacting to the racket and the assortment of unpleasant physical irritations (fever, aches, sore throat, nausea, itching, stinging, pounding sound, and exhaustion). It would be impossible to achieve a state of peace, let alone to concentrate on the math problems. This example may seem extreme, but children who have dysregulated nervous systems describe their experience in this way. While you might be slightly irritated by a car honking in traffic, your child might become hysterical and start screaming at the car doing the honking. The noise has created a sense of arousal (fear or anger) that is inconsistent with the event (honking), and the response that follows (screaming) is unusual and possibly confusing to those around the child.

Knowing that different individuals experience the world in unique ways helps us understand how people who have trouble processing, regulating, and modulating sensory information can become avoidant, anxious, impatient, irritable, or depressed, or what we call "dysregulated." Sensory dysregulation is common in children, and for decades, it has been called "sensory processing disorder" or "sensory integration dysfunction" by occupational therapy experts. Recently, psychologists have used the terms "sensory dysregulation" or "problems with sensory regulation" to describe how faulty processing of the sensory nervous system leads to negative emotions, beliefs, and behavior. Parents of children with sensory dysregulation are often confused or even frustrated by their child's behavior, because it does not make sense to them. Their child's behavior may be erratic, inconsistent, inappropriate, or downright strange for the given situation. In some cases, this behavior can even lead to or mimic childhood disorders such as anxiety disorders, oppositional defiant disorder, and a handful of others, which will be discussed later in this book.

The term "sensory integration dysfunction" was first used by occupational therapist Jean Ayres (1966, 1972) to identify and describe individuals with atypical responses to sensory stimulation, and it was later described in the book *The Out-of-Sync Child* by Carol Stock Kranowitz (2005). This clinical condition is now known as "sensory processing disorder" (SPD).

The concept of a dysregulation of the sensory system described in this book is identical to sensory processing disorder in terms of its mechanism, but "sensory dysregulation" also refers to the emotional and behavioral outcomes of a nervous system that is not functioning within the expected range. This book is not intended to replace or to diminish the work being done within the occupational therapy realm. In occupational therapy, the child is given many sensory experiences to help the nervous system become accustomed to different types of sensory input. This is very important work. Our focus here is an attempt to expand the understanding of the sensory system for parents and explain how it governs far more than just a child's reactions to certain stimuli.

This book describes how a child can learn, feel, and behave in unusual ways as a result of a glitch in the sensory system. More importantly, this book describes how parents can help their child cope with sensory glitches and understand their body and how it reacts. It explains how parents can change the way their child interacts with their environment and help them experience success in situations that have been challenging in the past. As a result, parents will learn to respond in healthier ways, which will improve both parent-child interactions and family functioning.

To illustrate what we are talking about with regard to nervous system regulation and how it affects children, we will use case examples throughout the book. We find that using real-life examples helps parents better understand what we are describing and relate it to their child's behavior. In the following example, Keesha represents a child who has problems with sensory regulation but also exhibits some unusual behaviors that are often misinterpreted by her teachers, parents, and friends. Keesha has what we call an under-responsive nervous system, one that senses things in a dampened way, less intensely than other children do. As a result, Keesha seeks stimulation and learns about her environment through exploration with her senses.

> Keesha is a five-year-old girl whose mother brought her in for evaluation after her kindergarten teacher expressed concerns about her unusual behavior. She reported that Keesha is constantly touching, rubbing, smelling, and licking objects in the classroom. She said, "It's as if Keesha does not know what an object is unless she has touched, smelled, and tasted it." The teacher said that Keesha has a hard time keeping her hands to herself and is constantly touching other students' hair or clothing during class, which disrupts the learning for the other students. In the cafeteria, she eats sardines and pickled herring while her tablemates cringe at the smells and try to move to other tables to get away from the noxious aromas. In class, Keesha is constantly moving, preferring to stand up rather than sit at her desk. Her teacher seemed frustrated and annoyed when speaking to Keesha's mother, who was well aware of her daughter's strange habits. Babies often put all sorts of things in their mouth, but Keesha continued doing this long after other children stop doing so, and she is always smelling and touching things. Keesha is a talkative, intelligent child who seems to want to do the right thing and to have friends, but she continues to engage in behaviors that get her into trouble, as if she does not care about the consequences. Keesha shows remorse for her actions but is

unable to consistently correct her behavior. Keesha does not meet criteria for autism or an autism spectrum disorder (ASD).

Keesha is a good example of a child with an under-responsive sensory nervous system, one who craves sensory input through smell, taste, movement, and touch in a more excessive way than is usual. Because her nervous system is under-responsive, she does not experience sensations such as touch, taste, or smell in way another child would, causing her to seek out more and more sensory input just to feel normal. Many people around her might think she is acting out or suffering from an emotional disorder—or is simply rude or misbehaved—but in reality, her behavior is just the result of her seeking knowledge and comfort. She is simply trying to learn about her environment and calm her nervous system down.

Problems with sensory regulation can cause not only obvious social difficulties, as is the case with Keesha, but also interpersonal difficulties that are subtler and harder to identify and that may be misunderstood by other people. The following is an example of how poor sensory regulation affects the relationships of a fourth-grade boy with a sensitive nervous system in a much more elusive way.

Ten-year-old Jose was having trouble with his friends. He had always had a small group of close friends who understood his lack of eye contact and his quirky nature and who were forgiving of his hot-and-cold reactions to seemingly benign situations. They usually handled it by giving him space, after which he would recover, and they would move on to the next game. Jose's friends liked to have sleepovers, but Jose did not like to go. He would get too tired and moody when he stayed all night. He used to go to "half-sleepovers," where he would stay until midnight, sleep at home, and return the next morning for breakfast. That worked when Jose was in third grade, but once he was a little older, he wanted to be close to his friends all night. He decided to start sleeping the whole night with his friends. Late nights watching movies and playing games left Jose sleep-deprived, grumpy, edgy, and overstimulated the next morning. He would pick fights with his friends and accuse them of purposely leaving him out of a joke or making fun of him, and this would make him the center of "drama" that would last for days. In addition, breakfast the next morning often included foods that had strong odors, such as bacon and eggs, which Jose did not eat, and the noise of the boys talking all at the same time was overwhelming to him. Jose started to feel different from his friends, like an outsider. He was sure that they were talking about him behind his back, which made him mad. He stopped playing basketball with them after school and avoided talking to them in the halls at school. Jose's friends were confused and did not understand why he stopped hanging out with them. His friends eventually stopped asking Jose to hang out, and they drifted apart.

Even by kid standards, Jose's reaction to the sleepover seems extreme. Jose was unable to effectively interpret social interactions because he has difficulty integrating multiple stimuli: being physically tired, the intense smell of the food, keeping up with the banter in the morning at breakfast, and the subtle social cues. In combination, all of these stimuli contributed to Jose's confusion about his friends' behavior and resulted in his experiencing intensely hurt feelings. In addition, because Jose does not make good eye contact, he missed the subtle cues and facial expressions that help give context to a conversation. Rather than talking to his friends about his feelings, Jose withdrew socially and shut down emotionally. His faulty assumptions perpetuated his hurt feelings, and his avoidance of social interactions contributed to a sense of isolation. Jose was also unable to calm himself down or talk to his friends about his feelings.

Accurately decoding situations contributes to emotional stability and regulation. The decoding process is an intrinsic function of the sensory system. Faulty decoding led Jose to misunderstand his friends' behavior. This misunderstanding caused him to assume that his friends must have been talking about him behind his back or possibly even making fun of him. In addition to a faulty understanding of his social environment, which made him anxious and angry, Jose lacked the skills to manage those overwhelming feelings. His emotional response was intense and confusing, which made him want to avoid similar experiences and ultimately caused him to withdraw from engaging in other relationships. Jose's response to sleepovers is a good example of how a normal event can become a catalyst for emotional dysregulation and problematic behavioral responses that can have long-lasting implications.

Another characteristic of children who have difficulties regulating their nervous systems is that they tend to have rigid mind-sets or patterns of thinking. In other words, they are inflexible in either their thinking or their behavior. We like to call this "raw spaghetti," because when you bend raw spaghetti, it breaks. Cooked spaghetti, on the other hand, is flexible. When kids who have over-responsive or under-responsive nervous systems are challenged, particularly when they are experiencing a reaction to a sensory experience, they often "break" and have a meltdown. Teaching kids to think in flexible ways is important in helping them become more adaptive and better-functioning people. Kids who are inflexible tend to think in black-and-white terms: things are good or bad, right or wrong, happy or sad, and so forth. We will talk more about ways to change these rigid mind-sets in a later chapter, but for now it is important to know that helping kids with over- or under-responsive nervous systems to think and behave in more flexible ways is a large part of helping these kids be successful in a multitude of situations.

Children with autism and autism spectrum disorders (ASD) are often plagued by poor sensory regulation and patterns of rigid thinking. If your child has been diagnosed with ASD, the information in this book will be one tool to help you understand their sensory experience, and it will provide useful information for helping them improve sensory regulation. People with ASD have issues in other domains in addition to the sensory, of course, but we will be discussing only the sensory realm in this book. Just be aware that this resource is one tool to help you understand your child and that there are many other books and resources available for parents of children with autism and ASD.

Whether or not your child has received a formal diagnosis, problems with sensory regulation can create confusion and disruption in the family, in school, and in friendships. Throughout this book we will help you explore the sensory functioning of each family member (yourself included), especially if one or more of your children exhibit disruptive, confusing, or reactive behaviors that are inconsistent with the situation. We will suggest exercises called "Take a Moment." These exercises are designed for you to think about yourself and your child and to make observations that will help you develop a better understanding of both yourself and your child.

This book is a tool to help you identify problems your child may have with sensory regulation and understand the function of your child's behavior as a result of these nervous system problems. In addition, it will teach you how to help your child develop skills to successfully regulate their nervous system and improve their functioning. The first part of the book provides an overview of sensory regulation and the various difficulties children and families experience when there are problems with either the intake or processing of sensory information. To do this, we give a brief explanation of the sensory nervous system and how it works, and we describe common behaviors in children who have problems with sensory regulation. We then explain how problems with sensory regulation can impact behavior and emotional and psychological functioning, and how it can, at times, even look like or be associated with other psychological problems in children. We then explore the common reactions parents have to their child's behavior and how parent responses can either help reduce or inadvertently encourage these problematic behaviors. Finding solutions that work for your child and your family is our goal.

The second part of the book focuses on giving you an array of useful tools to help your child cope with difficult sensory triggers. This will help your child learn to approach and get used to environments that may have previously been intolerable or may have been avoided. We will provide you with the essential ingredients for the recipe of sensory regulation—alternate ways to soothe, strategies for tolerating uncomfortable situations, and, most importantly, how to understand and have compassion for your child. Once your child learns to regulate their senses, you'll notice an improvement in the functioning of the entire family system. Our goals are to help you identify the specific sensory problems experienced by your child and develop compassion for your child and then to give you an arsenal of tools to help your child successfully manage their nervous system.

We recommend that you keep a journal as you work through this book. You can also download blank charts for repeated use at the website for this book: http://www.newharbinger.com/46264. There are numerous places in the book—in the Take a Moment exercises and elsewhere—where we recommend noting key things about your child and their response to the sensory world. A journal detailing your observations, insights, and memories will help you notice patterns in your child's behavior and in the reactions of others around your child. This knowledge is invaluable in your efforts to understand your child, as well as to help you determine what interventions seem to be the most effective for your child. It will also be a useful record if you ever pursue professional help for your child as it will give valuable information to the professional so that they can accurately understand your child's sensory nervous system.

So let's get started.

PART 1

Understanding Problems with Sensory Regulation

CHAPTER 1

Overview of the Senses
How Senses Affect Behavior

Jason is seven years old and a complete mystery to his parents. He has always been different from their other two children—harder to parent and almost impossible to please. As a baby and toddler, he was difficult to settle and did not sleep well. Now Jason is obstinate, strong-willed, and rigid in his thinking (if you say that the family is eating at Burger King and they end up at MacDonald's, look out!), and he will fly off the handle at the slightest frustration. At other times he is loving, kind, sweet to his siblings, helpful around the house, and eager to snuggle with his parents. Jason does not seem to respond to punishment, as if he does not care whether his privileges are revoked.

Socially, Jason has difficulty making and maintaining friendships, but he has a few close friends who have stuck by him since kindergarten. When he plays with other kids, he can be bossy and controlling, often causing others to back away from the game. He is a picky eater, hates to take showers, cannot stand to wear long pants, avoids new situations at all costs (especially if there are "unknowns"), and is terrified of loud noises such as fireworks, fire alarms, sirens, and concerts, which led to an additional diagnosis of specific phobia.

He has been diagnosed with ADHD and anxiety, has been prescribed numerous medications that never seem to work, and has seen a therapist for his anxiety. None of these interventions have resulted in any measurable improvements. The psychiatrist keeps switching medications, and the therapist is focused on trying to help Jason express his feelings through various means of play. Nothing seems to be helping, and his parents are getting increasingly frustrated with both the money they are spending and the lack of effort on Jason's part to improve his behavior.

Parenting is hard enough when behavior is predictable and age appropriate. When a child has problems regulating their nervous system, their internal experience can become so uncomfortable that it results in outward behavior such as crying, hiding, throwing tantrums, or refusing to participate, as well as unusual soothing behaviors such as licking, touching, smelling, and near constant movement. In the example of Jason, he might be viewed simply as a difficult child because of his extreme reactions to seemingly minor situations, but the truth is that his nervous system is wired a little differently, which affects how he feels and behaves.

Jason is terrified of loud noises because he is sensitive to sound, which means that a fireworks show actually hurts his ears rather than just sounding loud, as it does for most kids. His sound sensitivity also makes him nervous in new situations, as he does not know what sounds to expect. He prefers things that he is familiar with, which leads him to cling to rigid "rules" about what is and is not okay. Jason is also sensitive to touch and taste, which makes it hard for him to dress comfortably and hard for his parents to find food that he will eat, because his tastes are quite limited. Because of his sensory sensitivities, Jason has developed rigid expectations of how the world should be, reacting aggressively when life does not meet his predetermined expectations. Family members, teachers, and other people in Jason's life view his strong reactions and preferences as his being anxious, oppositional, and difficult, rather than simply responses to his distorted sensory experience.

As therapists, we have seen hundreds of children with emotional and behavioral difficulties, many of whom also struggle with these kinds of sensory differences. However, if we do not ask the right questions, this aspect of a child can be missed, and therefore the child's behavior is not fully understood, which makes successful treatment difficult. In this chapter, we hope to demystify the sensory system, helping you understand how your child's nervous system functions and, most importantly, how it drives tastes, preferences, choices, beliefs, and behaviors. In an effort to avoid discomfort or seek sensory experiences that provide comfort, children with sensory regulation problems can behave in ways that look like avoidance, irritability, oppositional behavior, anger, anxiety, or withdrawal, or they can exhibit unusual behaviors that just do not make sense given the circumstance.

When problems with sensory regulation are not identified, parents, professionals, and even children can become confused and frustrated. Children may be labeled "anxious," "difficult," or "challenging," landing them in therapy that may not be effective or in classrooms that are less challenging and therefore inappropriate for their ability level. Worse yet, these children may perceive themselves as "bad kids" who make bad decisions. Understanding your child's nervous system is often the key to understanding their behavior, particularly when the behavior is erratic, confusing, or unpredictable.

Before describing how sensory issues can impact a child's functioning, we will give a brief, simplified review of the nervous system and the different functions that are managed within this system. Understanding how the nervous system works will help you identify the glitches in your child's sensory system. Simply understanding why behaviors occur helps you develop tolerance and ultimately compassion and patience toward your child's difficult behaviors. That is the first step in this process and the focus of this chapter.

Overview of the Nervous System

The nervous system sends electrical signals to different areas of the body to coordinate voluntary and involuntary actions, such as walking (voluntary) and digestion (involuntary), based on information received both from within the body and from its interaction with the environment. The nervous system encompasses two main parts: the central nervous system and the peripheral nervous system. The central nervous system consists of the brain and the spinal cord, which evaluate incoming information and use it to give directions to the body. The peripheral nervous system is made up of bundles of nerves in the sense organs (eyes, nose, ears, skin, and mouth) that receive information from the environment. The peripheral nervous system relays this information to the central nervous system, which then tells the body what to do (put on a sweater if you feel cold air, plug your ears if you're walking past a noisy construction site, or cover your nose when smelling bad odors like a garbage truck passing by). Most human behavior is the result of information received through the sensory system.

> **Take a Moment:** Stop reading for a moment and notice what you sense—what noises, smells, and touch sensations are in your environment? In addition to the external sensations, do you notice any internal sensations, such as hunger or thirst? Now think about your movements, what are you doing? Have you scratched an itch, adjusted your clothing or posture, crossed or uncrossed your legs, taken a drink of water, or fiddled with something in the past few minutes? If so, why did you do this? What is your body telling you that causes you to react? Now, set a timer for five minutes and try to sit still. Notice whether your body is sending signals to move, scratch, or change something. During these five minutes, try not to respond to these urges—try to remain still. How does that feel? Are you able to sit with these sensations and not respond to them? Can you feel that itch and not scratch it? Do these sensations get stronger as you sit with them, or do they fade away? After the five minutes ends, write down your experience in your journal to help you remember how hard it can be to experience sensations and not respond to them.

Most human behavior is generated as a result of both internal and external sensory information. From moment to moment, our bodies are constantly in search of a sense of "feeling good," whether it is satisfying hunger or thirst, taking a nap, or drinking a cup of coffee for a boost of energy. We all assume that everyone's bodies read sensations in the same way, but do we? Do you see the color blue in the same way that someone else sees the color blue? Are we all on the same page in terms of how we translate sensations? We know that the answer is no. In fact, some people translate sensory information in extreme ways, leading to unusual behaviors. This actually explains a lot if you think about it. It explains why some children gravitate toward contact sports while others prefer solitary play. It explains why some children like spicy food and others prefer blander foods. It also explains subtle differences in behavior, such as why some children cannot sit completely still and must move some part of their bodies at all times (leg bobbling, finger tapping, fidgeting), while others are able to sit quietly for periods of time with no problem. Think about your child—what do you notice about them that is unique, different, or challenging?

Arousal and Calming

In addition to these moment-to-moment sensations and responses, the nervous system performs two important functions: arousal and calming. Arousal is a heightened sense of awareness, like when you are alone at night and you hear a strange noise, causing all of the senses to come to attention. Arousal is governed by the *sympathetic nervous system* and is responsible for reactions such as excitement, fear, and self-protection (becoming highly alert or vigilant). Think about the sympathetic nervous system as an internal "watchdog" that is always on alert for anything that might be dangerous or require increased energy. Calming is regulated by the *parasympathetic nervous system* and is the process of reducing arousal or settling the body, like how you feel after a great meal when you have nothing to do on a Sunday afternoon. The parasympathetic nervous system is also responsible for internal functions such as digestion and falling asleep. Different from the watchdog, the parasympathetic nervous system can be considered the "comfort dog," one that is focused on calming and reducing energy.

These two systems, arousal (sympathetic nervous system) and calming (parasympathetic nervous system), work together to make sure that a person's needs are being met at all times, such as staying safe from harm, eating when hungry, and resting when tired. They are also involved in how you regulate your body and maintain a sense of equilibrium or balance in response to internal and external stimuli, as we discussed in the introduction of this book.

These two regulatory systems keep the body balanced—most of the time. When the senses detect that something is out of balance, a message is sent to correct the imbalance. We have all experienced being out of balance at some point in our lives (for example, feeling hungry and low on energy or feeling stressed after a long day). When feeling out of balance, we naturally look to external sources to help our bodies regain equilibrium, both straightforward things, like getting a glass of water in response to feeling thirsty, and more subtle things, like taking a hot bath in the evening after a long day or going for a long walk in the park (both of which help decrease stress and increase a sense of calm).

Take a Moment: Think about a time when you were (or felt like you were) in a crisis situation, like when a fire alarm went off in a building or when you were watching a scary movie. How did your body feel? What did you notice about how your body responded to the crisis? Maybe you noticed your heart rate increase, your muscles get tense, and your energy surge. You may even have felt light-headed. This is a state of high arousal. Now think about a more common arousal experience, like when the phone rings or when you happen to see an old friend in the street. These are also states of arousal, but more moderate. What did they feel like? Did you feel energy or alertness? Were there emotions attached to those experiences? Now think about a time when you felt calm, like when you were about to fall asleep or when you just finished a hot bath. What did that feel like? Were your muscles relaxed? Did you breathe more slowly and deeply? Was your heart rate slow? Were there emotions attached to that experience?

What happens if there is a glitch in one or more of the senses and how they perceive information? What happens if the central nervous system is receiving information that is perceived inaccurately, either over-perceived or under-perceived? Think about perception as a continuum ranging from mild to extreme in terms of sensory sensation. If a child is on the mild end, they would be under-perceiving the sensation (for example, not being able to smell something that other people can smell, and only being able to smell strong odors). On the other end of the spectrum would be a child who over-perceives sensations (for example, a child who can smell even very slight odors and who finds strong odors overpowering and is constantly assaulted by smell). In the middle of the spectrum is the range of normal sensation, where many children fall. When the system receives information that is perceived to be too much (extreme) or too little (mild) given the circumstance, there is a reaction.

If a child bites into a sandwich and the mustard on the sandwich tastes like spicy hot sauce and feels like it is burning their mouth, they might tear up, spit out the bite, or cry in pain. If a new pair of jeans feels like it is made of sandpaper, the same child might immediately take them off. These are appropriate responses to what the child is experiencing, but if a parent does not realize that their child has this sensory difference, they might become confused or frustrated. The peripheral nervous system is misperceiving what is happening in the environment (the mustard is actually mild, and the jeans are quite soft and smooth) and delivering this misperceived information to the central nervous system for action.

Have you ever experienced a time when you misinterpreted something, like a balloon popping that you think is a gunshot or a stick in the leaves at the side of a path that you mistake for a rattlesnake, causing you to jump? You likely did not even think about it—you just reacted instantaneously. This is the central nervous system responding to misread information in an effort to protect you from potential harm. While you may be able to laugh at your reaction and correct yourself after you look closely and see that the "snake" is really just a stick, your child may not understand that their reaction is unnecessary—they might see the response as helpful. Your child may interpret this response as necessary and correct, given the stimulus. It would be as if you looked at the stick and continued to think that it was a rattlesnake.

In addition to responding to the information in the moment (spitting out the bite of the sandwich with burning-hot mustard and taking off the jeans that feel like sandpaper), children learn from these experiences and apply this learning to the future. From then on, this child might refuse to eat sandwiches with mustard—or might refuse to eat sandwiches at all—just to be safe. They might balk at wearing jeans in the future or eventually refuse to wear long pants at all to maintain a sense of comfort.

In addition to avoiding unpleasant experiences, children learn to do things that feel good to them. Tasting chocolate for the first time might lead to extreme pleasure, causing that child to seek chocolate in the future. Similarly, if biting and sucking on the collar of their shirt feels calming, a child would not hesitate to do this each time they need to feel calm. If visual clutter is stimulating for a child, dumping the entire box of a two-thousand-piece puzzle onto the floor might seem like a great solution to feeling bored. This chapter will help you begin to view your child's behavior differently, as adaptive responses given the presenting situations.

The Sympathetic Nervous System and Sensory Regulation

Our nervous systems are still performing their age-old duties. During evolution, humans developed the sympathetic nervous system response of arousal to survive in a dangerous world of predatory animals—to either fight the animal or run and seek shelter from the animal. Even though most of us do not have to worry about the presence of lions and tigers in our everyday lives, that sympathetic nervous system response still exists in our bodies. Imagine that you're walking across the street, and all of a sudden a car comes around the corner, speeding toward you. You would likely spring into action and jump out of the way. In order to act in time, this response would take place without any conscious thought. This sudden reaction might also be accompanied by involuntary responses from your sympathetic nervous system, such as rapid heartbeat, tense muscles, increased blood flow to internal organs, and an adrenaline rush. This arousal response is called the fight-flight-or-freeze response, and it serves an important, life saving function.

When sensory input is interpreted to be intensely unpleasant, the sympathetic nervous system can get triggered, resulting in the fight-flight-or-freeze response to non-dangerous triggers, such as a balloon popping, the taste of mustard, or the sensation of jeans on the legs. These non-dangerous triggers give rise to the same response that would occur if something dangerous were present. The heart still beats faster, muscles still tense, blood flow still increases, and adrenaline still gets boosted, causing the child to experience the fear response, not just discomfort. This explains why you may see your child have a strong reaction when asked to eat, drink, smell, or participate in something that other children do easily. The behavior of screaming might be considered a fight response. The behavior of avoiding—or even actually running away—would be a flight response. Finally, the behavior of shutting down and crying helplessly might be a freeze response. In any of these cases, the sympathetic nervous system is telling the child that the situation (the trigger) is dangerous, regardless of whether they know better. These behaviors can look like oppositional behavior, anxiety, or helplessness and are often misunderstood, even sometimes being labeled as a childhood behavioral disorder.

> Joly is a seven-year-old girl who lives with her family near a large lake. Her family owns a boat, and they love to go boating, fishing, and waterskiing in the summer—all except Joly. She has never liked the boat. In fact, she screams, becomes hysterical, cries, and hyperventilates when they even talk about taking a boat ride. At first her parents made her go, hoping she would get used to it. Instead, it began causing intense family conflict. Her brothers teased her, her parents punished her (and her brothers, when they found out that the boys were teasing her), and Joly felt sad about all of it. After years of struggles, her parents resorted to hiring a babysitter to stay with Joly when they went boating, because her reactions were too much trouble. Joly was relieved to not have to go on the boat but missed time with her family, because they were regularly out on the boat without her.

Joly has several nervous system issues going on here. The movement of the boat unsettles her nervous system, triggering the sympathetic nervous system response, making her body believe that she is in danger, like she is falling off a cliff. She also experiences the sensation of wind against her skin as painful. She feels her hair blowing against her face as if whips were thrashing her skin. Finally, the noise of the boat is painful to her ears, making the whole experience completely intolerable. The experience of being on a boat is so unpleasant that it triggers both the fight and flight responses in her body, which look like anger and refusal to participate.

Another important thing to know about the brain is that when the fight-flight-or-freeze response is activated, the frontal cortex of the brain shuts down. The frontal cortex helps with executive functioning and problem solving, so when it shuts down, the person is unable to think clearly. This is why when people are in a panic, such as when a fire breaks out in a shopping mall, you see people running madly about, trampling one another, or freezing without thinking to do seemingly obvious things like exiting the building calmly, helping other people, or calling 911. When a child's sympathetic nervous system gets triggered, even in response to a sensory experience, they may respond in irrational, if not hysterical, ways, like Joly. Later, you may see them calm down and apologize for their behavior, but they might not be able to explain why they reacted the way they did. This is actually the result of the frontal cortex shutting down due to the fight-flight-or-freeze response and losing the capacity to think clearly in that moment.

The Parasympathetic Nervous System and Sensory Regulation

Remember that there are two systems at work in the nervous system, the arousal and the calming systems—or the sympathetic and parasympathetic systems. While the sympathetic nervous system response of fight, flight, or freeze is important in sensory regulation, so is the parasympathetic system, that of calming. Children engage in calming activities to soothe their nervous systems all the time. Children use thumb sucking, snuggling against a mother's chest, or rubbing a soft blanket when they are trying to calm themselves. You typically see these behaviors when your child is trying to fall asleep, when they are at rest (watching television or reading a book), or after a stressful experience. Think about your child and the things they have done over the years to soothe themselves, as well as what you have done to soothe them. Maybe there were things that you learned to do to calm your child down, such as rubbing their feet, driving them around in the car seat, singing softly, or bouncing them gently while holding them in your arms to help them settle down.

For children who experience sensory information a bit differently, they may seek alternate, more unconventional, forms of calming behaviors. Some children feel calmed by spinning in circles, touching their private parts, seeing their toys lined up in a certain order, or even pulling out their hair. What looks like strange or harmful behavior might actually be your child's attempt to regulate their dysregulated body.

> Devon is seven years old and has started to engage in some behaviors that are alarming to his parents. He has been twisting his hair until it is in a knot, then pulling out the hair. His parents noticed the bald spots on his scalp, which was shocking. They noticed that he engages in this behavior while in bed at night, while watching television in the afternoon, and after being in a place that is highly stimulating (like a day in school, the mall, or a playdate with a friend). They do not see the behavior when he is engaged in play, when he is in social situations, or when he is moving around.

Hairpulling is a fairly common self-soothing behavior in children and is a good example of one that appeals to children who have a different experience of the sensory nervous system. As you can see with Devon, his body gets stimulated and needs calming, either after being in a highly stimulating environment or before going to sleep. Devon seeks this calming sensation through pulling his hair, a behavior that he has learned, through trial and error, works really well to settle his nervous system. He also finds it interesting to look at the hair bulb at the end of the strand (visual) and enjoys rubbing it along his face (tactile), both of which are calming sensations to Devon. Most people would view hairpulling as strange, self-harm behavior that signifies great pathology, when in actuality, it is a self-soothing behavior that works quite well to induce calm for some, very much like how thumb sucking functions for small children. The results of hairpulling (hair loss, feeling unable to control their own behavior, and social reactions from peers) are actually the main concerns with this behavior and why it is worth treating in the therapy office. So, the parasympathetic nervous system response (calming) is as important as the sympathetic (arousal) when understanding your child's nervous system and behavior. Understanding what is driving a behavior is a key ingredient to being a strong advocate for your child.

Sensory regulation problems are a breakdown in some part of the sensory system that results in unusual emotional and behavioral responses. Beyond situational likes and dislikes, sensory symptoms may also cause anxiety, as described in the example of Joly. Her experience of movement, sound, and wind was so intensely uncomfortable that she responded with fear and avoidance of boats. Intellectually, she made sense of this by telling herself "I hate boats," when in reality, she does not like the movement, the sensation of the wind, and the noise associated with boats. Devon, on the other hand, displays self-soothing behaviors (hairpulling and twisting) that alarmed his parents.

Unusual behaviors in children are oftentimes an attempt to avoid unpleasant sensory experiences or to soothe their agitated nervous systems. Your child may be coping with uncomfortable sensory stimuli either by reacting to or avoiding certain situations or by engaging in self-soothing behaviors that can seem unusual to you. Sensory reactivity can lead to predictable behaviors, which may help you understand why your child behaves the way they do. Think about your child and their behavior— what do they do to calm themselves? Has your child ever engaged in what seemed like an unusual behavior to you, one that would not necessarily feel soothing to you?

Information Gathered by the Nervous System Leads to Learning and Behavior

How a child experiences sensations leads to how they respond to them, both emotionally and behaviorally. These experiences lead to learning, memory, and future behavior. Learning takes place every day, especially in young children—they learn that a lollipop tastes sweet (*I like lollipops*), that their teddy bear is soft (*the teddy bear makes me feel good*), and that Grandpa smells like menthol (*I think Grandpa smells weird*). Behavior, such as asking for the lollipop, seeking the teddy bear, or avoiding giving Grandpa a big hug, may result from this learning process.

Learning also applies to children who have sensitivities in their nervous systems, which can lead to problems in behavior. A girl who has a very sensitive nose and cannot tolerate some smells may learn to avoid certain places, like the school cafeteria. Without any knowledge that her sensory experiences differ from those of her peers, she may generalize this avoidance to other places, like certain restaurants, public restrooms, or fish markets. For her parents, this might make routine outings quite difficult. One could say that this child *learned* that she did not like these specific places and behaved accordingly, just like a child with typical sensory functions *learns* not to touch a hot stove.

Similarly, a boy who perceives clothing to feel itchy, tight, and very uncomfortable may agree to wear only a few articles of clothing in his closet (maybe only loose-fitting and extremely soft T-shirts and shorts). As a result, this child's clothing choices may be profoundly limited and seem almost compulsive. Buying new clothes or broadening the wardrobe may seem impossible to his parents, and arguments over having to wash some clothes daily can become commonplace. This child *learned* that only certain items of clothing are comfortable, and these items become the only options that are acceptable to him.

When the sympathetic nervous system is triggered, learning is powerful and immediate. One only has to see a video of a lion successfully hunting a zebra to learn that the lion is a potentially dangerous animal!

Think about a situation that is less obvious, like a dog barking at the postal worker. Every day that the postal worker drops off the mail, the dog barks ferociously, and after the person leaves, the dog stops barking. The dog perceives danger (even though the postal worker has never done harm to the dog or the dog's family) and behaves in a manner that is intended to scare off the perceived threat. When the postal worker leaves (because the mail has been delivered), the dog likely has "learned" that the barking has successfully scared off the "intruder" and that danger is now reduced. The dog believes that it has saved their family from potential harm, so that barking is likely to occur the next time the postal worker delivers the mail.

This example illustrates how learning can be powerful, but faulty. This dog likely believes that they have scared off a dangerous intruder, but the postal worker is not dangerous, and there never was any danger to ward off. This is how it works with the sensory nervous system; a child perceives danger with a sensory trigger and behaves to reduce the danger, believing, in the end, that danger has been avoided. Fortunately, most sensory triggers are not interpreted to the extreme of being dangerous in a life-threatening way—they just become preferences, likes and dislikes that help develop our sense of self.

Examining Your Own Nervous System

A well-functioning nervous system gathers all pertinent information from all of the sensory sources, integrates it effectively, and then makes decisions that lead to system harmony. Sensory perceptions determine likes and dislikes in every way imaginable—for example, decorating a house in a style that is pleasing to the eye, wearing perfume that is pleasing to the nose, listening to music that is pleasing to the ear, and so on. Each of us may have a different idea about what is satisfying to us, and our unique nervous system guides each of us to create a personally gratifying environment that suits our sensibilities.

The nervous system's responses let us know about our preferences—what we like and dislike. A loud rock concert is intolerable for some people, and spicy foods may be inedible for others. Avoiding certain foods or loud music are just a couple examples of how the nervous system learns what is comfortable and what is unpleasant or offensive and helps us make decisions accordingly. Think about your own life—are there situations that you avoid or dislike, even though you are not quite sure why? Maybe you don't like a certain section of the grocery store because it is cold or has a fishy smell. Maybe you avoid loud concerts or noisy restaurants. Maybe Disney World was a nightmare as you endured those rides with your child, causing you to feel nauseous afterward. To fully appreciate the uniqueness of your child and their nervous system, it is important for you to get to know your own nervous system. Sensory regulation problems seem to run in families, and we find that it is common for one or both parents to also have strong sensory likes and dislikes, many of which they did not realize were there.

Take a Moment: Take a moment to think about your nervous system. What do you like, and what do you dislike? Are there any foods that you really cannot eat because of the way they taste, smell, or feel in your mouth? Are there smells that you are repulsed by (outside of the obvious ones)? Are there any tactile sensations that really bother you? What kinds of clothes do you prefer, given their pattern, color, texture, or snugness of fit? What soothes you or calms you down? If you were to create a room that was completely soothing and relaxing to you, what would be in it? (Would it be a sunny room or one with windows that don't face the sun? Would there always be a vase of sweet-smelling flowers, or would it be a kitchen, smelling of roasted chicken or a rich pasta sauce? Bright white walls or soft yellow or deep blue? Music playing or just the sounds of nature coming in from outside? Would it be full of artwork and books and knickknacks, or would it be simple and Spartan? Is there anything that you absolutely would ban from your room?) In the Netherlands there are multisensory environments (MSE) called *Snoezelen* rooms that are tailored to soothe the nervous system of the individual living in that house. If you could create a *Snoezelen* room in your house, what would it be like? Think of the colors, textures, smells, sounds, and tastes that you might put there. Read through the below list of common preferences to help you identify your individual likes and dislikes. Make notes in your journal about yourself and your unique preferences.

- *Touch:* soft, squishy, cool, stretchy, sticky, furry, fuzzy, rough, scratchy, tight fitting, spiky, smooth, bumpy, wet, warm—think of the textures of burlap, velvet, chenille, wool, silk, satin, and linen.

- *Smell:* sweet or fruity (like flowers, vanilla, cinnamon, lavender, orange, citrus, peppermint, rose, or chocolate), woody (a forest in the mountains or eucalyptus), chemical (ammonia or bleach), toasted or nutty (fresh bread), pungent (blue cheese or smoke), or decayed (spoiled milk).

- *Sound:* nature sounds (birds, insects chirping, rain, leaves rustling, a babbling stream, a thunderstorm, or waves on a beach), music (classical, rock, country, jazz), talking, white noise, silence, tones with no melody, a clock ticking, the sound of a train, sounds of a busy city, humming, loud noises, soft noises, the chewing of food.

- *Visual:* light colors, dark colors, bright colors, solids, stripes, patterns (plaid or paisley), dim lights, bright lights, whites, monochromatic, multicolor, busy patterns, block patterns, geometric patterns, soft flowing patterns, polka dots, patterns of lines, holes on things, bumpy-looking texture, smooth-looking texture, subtle-looking texture, animal prints.

- *Taste:* general tastes (sweet, salty, sour, savory, spicy or hot, fishy, meaty, bitter) or specific tastes (cinnamon, rosemary, truffle, vanilla, coconut, chocolate, mint).

Now that you have identified your sensory preferences, compare them with those of another family member or your spouse. Oftentimes people within the same family have very different preferences, sometimes causing conflict. Notice if there are any likes and dislikes that you did not realize you had, perhaps that you did not think were different from others. Maybe you assumed that all people felt the same way about a certain smell or texture. Now imagine how alone and confused your child may feel not realizing that they may smell, hear, see, taste, and experience things differently than other people.

Remember Jason? Through self-reflection, his parents learned that they both enjoy adventure, new experiences, and getting the most out of every weekend. They could not understand why Jason refused to go to festivals, ride amusement-park rides, or eat at new and unusual restaurants. Jason, who has a sensitive nervous system, needs quiet time and reading for several hours on the weekend; he needs structure and predictable outings and ones that do not involve crowds, loud noises, and strong-flavored food. Once Jason's parents became aware of his sensory issues, they enrolled him in an art class on Saturdays that was quiet and where he could create art to his liking. While he was at art class, they would have their adventures, allowing him to have a more relaxed experience. Jason's parents allowed him to choose the restaurant when they went out together, and they celebrated his choices. In the past they had assumed that he also needed movement, adventure, and excitement without realizing that what he really needed was quiet time each weekend to offset the busy school week. They began making quiet time a significant part of the weekend schedule.

Jason was not trying to cause a problem; he was simply reacting to an imbalance in his nervous system. He could not tolerate the "chaos" of the adventures his parents were creating for the family and was seeking calm after a long week—he needed that to stay in balance. Most importantly, Jason really enjoyed the art class, which helped him feel happier and less irritable during the weekend. This is a good example of how simple changes can lead to greater understanding and better functioning for the entire family.

Conclusion

In this chapter, we reviewed the sympathetic nervous system, which is responsible for self-protection in response to danger, and how it can be triggered by strong stimuli, resulting in anxious reactions to seemingly harmless sensations. We reviewed how reactions in the sympathetic nervous system can lead to faulty learning and beliefs, which is confusing to parents and is often misunderstood (they think their child is acting out or defiant). We reviewed how the parasympathetic nervous system is responsible for calming, and that for some children, calming looks very different than it does for most people, and it can even look like bizarre or inappropriate behavior. The goal of this chapter is to help you begin to understand how the neurology of the brain and how each child is wired determines a multitude of preferences, beliefs, and behaviors. In the next chapter, we will go a little deeper into the functions of the brain and how glitches in the nervous system might affect your child and their functioning.

CHAPTER 2

A Better Understanding of Your Child's Behavior
The Specifics of Sensory Regulation Problems

Before you can truly understand your child's behavior, it is important to understand a little more specifically how sensory information is processed in the brain and specific problems that can arise when all systems are not functioning properly. We are not saying that your child's brain has something wrong with it, but that there might be glitches in how information is taken in, understood, processed, or retrieved, causing issues in their behavior. We will also go through each of the senses and explain what it looks like when one of the senses is either over- or under-responsive. First, let's take a look at how all of the sensory information is modulated in the brain—how the brain manages the multitude of sensory information that is taken in every second of the day.

Sensory Modulation

The central nervous system regulates all sensory input and makes decisions about appropriate responses based upon the information it receives from the senses. The central nervous system is like the manager of a company. The manager relies on the many workers beneath them to give accurate information about different aspects of the functioning of the company. Once information is collected, the manager makes decisions about what to do. If the workers report that sales are up, the manager might buy more inventory to keep up with sales and avoid running out of a certain product. If, however, the worker is not reporting accurate information to the manager—maybe the worker says that sales are up, when really they are down—buying more inventory will result in a surplus of product, which could cause significant problems for the company. Accurate information is critical for the functioning of the company. Likewise, when there are problems with sensory modulation, sensory information is not being read accurately, thus misinformation is being delivered to the central nervous system. When a child perceives sensations differently than other children, we say they have problems with *sensory modulation*. There are two main subtypes of sensory modulation that have been identified:

- *Sensory over-responsive:* that sense is experienced in a much more intense manner than others would perceive it, causing a child to over-respond to the situation.

- *Sensory under-responsive:* that sense is experienced in a much less intense manner than others might experience it, causing a child to require more input to register the sensation.

Think about modulation or perception as a continuum ranging from over-responsive to under-responsive, with "normal" being somewhere in the middle. Each of the senses can be placed on a continuum from over- to under-responsive (see image below). Think about how your senses fall on this continuum for each of these senses. Think about your child as well; how do they fall on the different continuums?

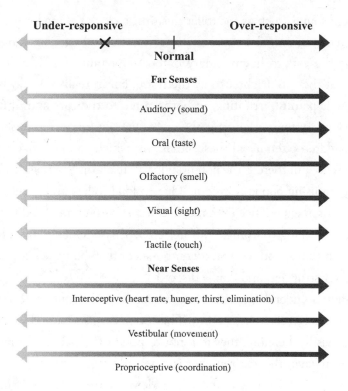

This next section will provide an overview of each sense and what an over-response and under-response might look like. Let's see how over-responsive and under-responsive kids look across the near and far senses. Remember, each sense can be calibrated separately, so do not assume that because your child is over-responsive to one sense that they will be over-responsive to all senses. As you read through the following descriptions, think about your child and how they react to certain sensory stimuli.

Far Senses

Auditory Sense: Children who are over-responsive to noise hear sounds louder than other children. As a result, they typically do not like loud, unexpected noises. They may cover their ears, scream, or cry when they hear fireworks, a fire alarm, or a car honking. In addition, common household sounds such as the toilet flushing, a clock ticking, or the sound of a lawn mower may also cause extreme discomfort. Reactions range from covering the ears to having angry outbursts or tantrums. Children will report that they are frightened by the noise, but in reality, it may be that the noise is painful, irritating, or bothersome to the ears and ultimately the nervous system, triggering the fight-flight-or-freeze response. As a result, children often avoid these situations, which can look like refusing to go to school (if there is the potential for a fire alarm or a noisy cafeteria) or avoiding using public restrooms (due to loud toilets and hand dryers). Some children experience extreme discomfort with certain bodily sounds (chewing, slurping, burping, sniffing, etc.); this is called "misophonia." Children may respond with angry outbursts or irritability, leading to conflict, power struggles, and family discord.

Children under-responsive to noise also have difficulty with auditory sensations, but in the opposite way. They do not register sound that others can hear easily, therefore, they may not respond to verbal cues or may talk loudly even when the environment is quiet, not registering the volume of their own voice. Children who are under-responsive may be confused about the origin of sounds or may say "what?" frequently. Finally, under-responsive children tend to gravitate toward loud music and lively, noisy environments. These children often are uncomfortable or misbehave in environments that are silent or require quiet behavior, such as classrooms, places of worship, movies, museums, and libraries.

Oral Sense: The over-responsive reaction to taste is fairly common in children and usually looks like picky eating. These children prefer bland, mostly unhealthy foods such as mac and cheese, chicken nuggets, and plain pasta, and often will reject most vegetables. Children with severe oral over-responsiveness have extreme reactions to food and will often only eat a few acceptable items. Eating foods with strong flavors—anything salty, sour, sweet, tangy, or spicy—may cause them to gag or vomit. In addition, these children may have a history of sucking, chewing, or swallowing problems in early childhood. If there is a history of swallowing problems leading to gagging or choking, anxiety about eating and choking can develop. In these cases, it is common for kids to limit their diet to soft, mushy foods that are unlikely, in their mind, to lead to choking.

Sometimes it is not the taste of the food, but the texture that is the problem—that is, not liking mushy or lumpy foods such as bananas or oatmeal. In addition, oral over-responsive children are often reluctant to brush and floss their teeth because of the strong taste of toothpaste or the feeling of the brush or floss against their teeth, tongue, and gums. Oral over-responsiveness can impact nutrition and growth (due to a limited diet), dental health (due to a lack of brushing and flossing), family dynamics (due to conflict), and social development (due to how eating affects the ability to socialize by going to dinner, eating at a friend's house, having limited food choices, etc.). In some more extreme cases, these children could develop or be diagnosed with avoidant restrictive food intake disorder (ARFID).

Oral under-responsive children seek out oral sensations, which can be alarming to parents. These children may lick, taste, or chew inedible objects (chewing on clothing or sucking on hair); they often love strong-flavored foods such as hot sauce, fishy-tasting fish like sardines, salty foods, or sour foods; they are felt to be a blessing to parents, because they will try foods that children typically shy away from. Sometimes these children have a history of sucking their thumb, even past the normal age of stopping, have a history of excessive drooling, and may chew on pens, pencils, or the inside of their mouth or tongue. Parents are typically concerned about oral-seeking behaviors for health-related reasons, such as contact with germs or potential choking hazards.

Olfactory Sense: Children who are over-responsive to smells are bothered or nauseated by strong or even mild smells. Parents may notice behavioral changes in situations that have unusual scents or on days that the house was cleaned with a strong-smelling cleanser. They may complain about or avoid places such as the school cafeteria, public restrooms, hospitals, or the zoo. Some children may notice subtle smells that others do not notice, such as a hint of rosemary, a whiff of perfume, or the chemical smell of a shirt that was recently purchased from a store.

Children who are under-responsive to smell tend to like certain smells, even if others find them offensive. These children repeatedly smell objects, especially if they find the smell interesting or strong. Oftentimes, when an object is first being inspected, a child will smell it once or twice before deciding whether they like it, even if the object does not appear to others to have any odor at all. Smell under-responsive children sometimes have difficulty telling the difference between smells or do not notice smells at all, even when others are reacting to them. They may like to eat foods with strong odors, such as sardines, which may be offensive to other children around them. Teenagers with this sensory under-responsiveness may not notice their own body odor or bad breath, and they can be reluctant to bathe or wear deodorant, causing feedback or reactions from family and peers.

Visual Sense: Children who are visually over-responsive notice visual things that other children do not. They may squint in bright sunlight or lights, may insist that things be ordered or arranged in certain ways (for example, they may want all shoes lined up in the closet to make it look nice), and often avoid making eye contact while talking. It is also common for them to be distracted by visual stimuli (oftentimes irrelevant), refuse to read books that have narrow margins and small fonts, prefer solid-colored clothing to stripes and patterns, fix wall hangings and framed pictures that are slightly crooked, and become overly aroused by brightly colored or visually busy rooms.

Visually under-responsive children are less likely to notice visual details, which can lead to trouble with reading (difficulty tracking objects or lines of a paragraph, skipping a line of text, or mixing up similar letters, such as *p*, *q*, *b*, and *d*). Other problems associated with being visually under-responsive include having too much focus on the details of a picture while missing the whole, difficulty identifying objects that are partially hidden, poor driving skills, trouble copying from the blackboard, and trouble reading maps. At home they have unusually cluttered rooms, can be disorganized and messy, and like bright colors and patterns.

Tactile Sense: Children who are tactile over-responsive are particular about the way things feel on their skin. Oftentimes these children avoid windy situations, such as riding in boats or convertibles, clothing that is not extremely soft, socks with seams, long pants, messy play (for example, finger painting or playing in sand or dirt), or cooking that involves touching food.

Behaviorally, they are reluctant to cuddle, dislike even light touches or soft kisses, have a very hard time wearing tight-fitting clothing or clothes that feel rough in texture, avoid wearing underwear, and do not like the feeling of sand under their feet. Parents can spend hours in the morning trying to get their child ready for school or bargaining with them to get dressed, resulting in being late for school, family conflict, and potential job disruption for parents (due to missed work). Many times these kids do not like the feeling of water on their skin, making baths or showers a focus of conflict, or seemingly enjoyable family activities out of the question, such as going to the beach or swimming pool (sand, water, and sunscreen). Most importantly, tactile sensitivities can interfere with the parent-child bonding process, particularly when children dislike being touched, kissed, or cuddled. Parents misunderstand this physical reluctance and take these responses personally, resulting in hurt feelings for both parent and child.

On the other end of the spectrum, tactile under-responsive children do not notice sensations of touch, which can lead to behaviors and reactions that look quite different. Many times these children do not realize that their hands or faces are dirty; they touch, tap, or rub objects in their environment; they may get bumped, hit, or scratched without noticing; and they may play too roughly with other children. Because these youngsters do not register sensations on the skin as others do, they may not notice that they are bleeding due to an injury or they may seek out seemingly painful experiences. Peers do not understand this "reckless" behavior, which can interfere with friendship and social development. Children who are under-responsive to touch receive a great deal of negative feedback or correction from the outside world ("Wash your hands!" "Stop rough-housing!". "Stop touching everything!"), resulting in complicated emotions for the child, who may feel chastised, misunderstood, and socially isolated.

Near Senses

Interoceptive Sense: Children who are over-responsive to the interoceptive sense tend to be acutely aware of their internal sensations, such as heart rate, hunger, thirst, or the need to go to the restroom. They may become frightened of the feeling of a rapidly beating heart, or they may overeat or drink too much to avoid the sensations of hunger and thirst. Because the interoceptive sense involves the elimination system, some children spend lots of time in the restroom or make many repeated trips to the restroom to avoid feeling the need to eliminate waste. Other children will delay going to the bathroom because the feeling of elimination itself is uncomfortable or even painful, causing constipation or frequent accidents with either stool or urine leakage. These children are misunderstood as having behavioral issues and can be diagnosed with encopresis (defecation accidents), enuresis (urination accidents), or oppositional defiant behavior.

In contrast, children who are under-responsive to internal sensations may not notice feelings of hunger or thirst or may seek out activities that increase their heart rate, such as vigorous exercise. Sometimes under-responsive children don't register feeling full and end up eating large quantities of food, leading to overeating and possibly obesity. It is common for them to not notice the need to eliminate waste and are therefore slow to potty train or have frequent accidents. Sometimes these children will enjoy the feeling of hunger and therefore skip meals to feel hungry. All of these behaviors can be confusing to and cause anxiety for parents.

Vestibular Sense: Children who are over-responsive to the vestibular sense do not like the feeling of movement. As a result, they will often avoid playgrounds and outings on boats and may become easily carsick. These children typically dislike swing sets, seesaws, bike riding, swimming, amusement parks, long car trips, heights, and carousels. These sensory dislikes may set them apart from other children and can interfere with friendship development. These children may appear to be cautious, frightened, or oppositional in environments that others see as fun, when in reality, they are simply reacting to certain types of movement.

By contrast, the vestibular under-responsive child craves all kinds of movement. These children never seem to sit still; they love to spin, jump, run, flip, and tumble, and are often thrill seekers. They shake their legs while sitting, tap their fingers, fidget, pick, wiggle, and are in constant motion. They stand out from their peers because of their activity level and demand for action and excitement. These children may be perceived as brave, adventuresome, hyperactive, or bold risk-takers.

Proprioceptive Sense: The proprioceptive over-responsive child has difficulty understanding where their body is in relation to other objects. These children often seem clumsy, bump into things, appear stiff, and are uncoordinated. They do not like other people to encroach on their space or even to touch their body, they have a rigid or tense posture, and they dislike stretching their limbs. These children may also fear that objects are closer than they appear so that they startle easily or have difficulty going up and down stairs, often skipping a step or falling. They tend to overreact when objects pass quickly by them, making learning to drive a challenge. These children also have a lot of difficulty playing sports that require an accurate understanding of spatial relations (catching and throwing), running, hitting or kicking a ball, or tackling and being tackled.

Under-responsive children will seek proprioceptive input—for example, they will take heavy steps while walking (banging their feet on the floor), like to sit with knees tucked under themselves, hyperextend joints such as fingers and knees, and bang body parts, such as clapping hands together or slapping their jaw with their hands. They love to be squished and to receive bear hugs, push hard when opening or closing doors, often misjudge the weight of an object, are known to accidently break objects, and frequently rip paper while erasing due to pressing too hard. These under-responsive children prefer tight clothing, love rough-housing, and may be unintentionally aggressive with other children. In addition, they prefer sports where there is physical contact, like football, basketball, and lacrosse.

> *Eight-year-old Aisha sits at the dinner table ready to eat. As often happens, Aisha erupts in anger at her mother because, in her opinion, she is chewing her food too loudly. Aisha can't stand it. She blames her mother for making her upset. She feels that her mother could chew in a way that doesn't bother her and is chewing loudly on purpose. She looks forward to meals and is always upset when she hears her mother's chewing noises. Her stomach tightens, she feels hot, and her heart begins to race. The sound is intolerable. Aisha suddenly stands up, yelling, "Stop chewing so loud!" Her mother is visibly upset, starts to cry silently, and attempts to quiet her chewing. Her father tells Aisha to go to her room and think about her behavior and how she has hurt her mother's feelings. Aisha goes to her room but secretly gets on her tablet to play her favorite game. The entire family begins to fear dinnertime, as it has become a battleground. Aisha's mother has started to cook Aisha's favorite meals most nights to appease her and hopefully make her less reactive to Mom's chewing.*

Aisha hears her mother's chewing as disgusting and loud because she is over-responsive to sound. She cannot focus on anything else but her mother's chewing. It causes her such discomfort that she cannot tolerate it and responds by yelling. Aisha is displaying the sympathetic nervous system's fight response, as if she had been sitting on a bed of ants. She's excruciatingly uncomfortable. Unfortunately, Aisha's reaction to this specific situation is intense and immediate, lashing out in anger so her mother will stop making the sound that is intolerable for her. This example illustrates how faulty modulation of sensory data (actually hearing the chewing more loudly than another person might hear it) can lead to emotional and behavioral dysregulation that affects the entire family.

Now you are starting to see how being over- or under-responsive to sensations can cause children to look anxious (through avoidance and fearful responses such a crying, hysteria, having to do things a certain way, and panic), oppositional (anger, irritability, or refusal to go places or eat foods), or downright strange (licking, smelling, tapping, rubbing, or other unusual behaviors). Without knowing about your child's nervous system, it is hard to fully understand what is driving their behavior.

Environmental Factors Can Affect Day-to-Day Behavior

Remember, each sense is unique and not predictive of the others—that is, a child may be overly sensitive to smell but may love hard touch. To add to the complexity, children may respond differently from day to day, due to different variables such as time of day, amount of sleep, the presence of peers, and other sensory aspects of the environment. It is not accurate to assume that a child is either over-responsive or under-responsive across all aspects of the sensory nervous system or across all environments.

Let's look back at Joly from chapter 1. Joly was uncomfortable on boats, as she experienced the wind as hurting her face and the movement of the boat as actually dangerous. Interestingly, after she learned more about her sensory responses, she learned how to take boat rides with her family without terrible discomfort. She was less stimulated early in the day, whereas later in the day (after school and soccer practice), her capacity to tolerate uncomfortable things was diminished, so boat rides in the morning were acceptable. In addition to changing the time of day, she was able to make modifications that also helped her tolerate the boat ride. Her dad driving slowly allowed her nervous system to get used to the movement, permitting her body to adjust. She was able to keep her hair from hitting her face with it bound in a ponytail and could reduce the sound of the motor by wearing noise-canceling headphones, all of which made a huge difference in how she felt on the boat. This illustrates how the nervous system can respond differently to the same sensory trigger, depending on the amount of stimulation that has occurred in a day and in response to minor adjustments to sensory irritations.

Sensory Processing

How the body experiences sensations by the peripheral nervous system (modulation), either over-responsive or under-responsive, determines whether the information is accurate. In addition to the accuracy of information, we also have to understand how information (accurate or inaccurate) is processed and organized by the brain or central nervous system before it is used to determine appropriate action. The brain gathers, organizes, interprets, and balances the flow of information coming into the central nervous system. Sensory problems, however, may not be with the perception of the sensation (modulation), but rather in the processing of it. Using the metaphor of the company referenced earlier in this chapter, the manager of the company is the brain and central nervous system. The manager relies upon information given to them by the peripheral nervous system (the workers). In the earlier example, bad information from the workers (poor modulation) can lead to poor decisions made by the manager. Conversely, the central nervous system or manager might get good information, but the manager has terrible skills at bookkeeping, accounting, or other business skills, leading to problems with the company as well. In the end, behavior may be unusual, but for a different reason.

Sensory processing has three three main responsibilities that can go wrong, thus leading to problems:

- *Inhibition:* to inhibit unnecessary responses by recognizing the information as nonessential or nonthreatening—for example, it stops us from screaming and running when a balloon is popped.

- *Habituation:* to acclimate or "get used to" sensations that are persistent or repetitive—for example, getting used to feeling the seatbelt across your body after being buckled for some time.

- *Discrimination:* to discriminate between different sensory stimuli—for example, being able to identify items by different shapes (a car versus a truck), textures (a beach towel versus a bathing suit), smells (cinnamon versus cayenne pepper), or other identifying sensory characteristics.

Let's take a look at each of these processes.

Inhibition

At any given moment, many messages are entering the brain and central nervous system through the eyes, ears, nose, mouth, skin, and internal organs, such as the stomach, bowels, bladder, heart, and lungs. In response to these many messages, inhibition helps the brain allow responses that are appropriate and stop or "inhibit" responses that are inappropriate when stimuli are nonessential or not dangerous. For example, a batter in baseball is supposed to focus on hitting the ball. They must inhibit responding to the heckling of the crowd at the ballpark. If they have poor inhibition, they will be distracted by the hecklers and might begin to scream back at them, telling them exactly what they think about them as well—or at least they will lose concentration on the ball and will be more likely to strike out.

A child who has trouble with inhibition may not be able to stop themselves from reacting to various (irrelevant) noises in a lively environment or may say whatever comes into their mind, even if it is not appropriate for the situation. In sum, these kids look impulsive and tend to react to sensations without thinking. Inhibition allows a child to stop and think before responding to a given stimulus. Children with poor inhibition are less able to stop and think, so the reaction that occurs can be inappropriate, unfiltered, or impulsive.

A very different manifestation of inhibition is a sort of "over-inhibition," in which a child becomes overly focused on one task while completely ignoring all other competing stimuli, such as eating, sleeping, or going to the bathroom. This type of over-focus or over-inhibition causes a child to appear zoned out or in a trance while engaged in an activity, making it difficult to get their attention or to get them to switch activities. Parents frequently see this with activities such as video games, where a child can focus on playing the game for hours without eating, drinking, or sleeping. Below is a list of behaviors that are common in children who have problems with inhibition. Do any of these behaviors sound familiar to your child?

- acting without thinking

- asking repeatedly for the same thing after being told no

- startling easily to noise

- startling easily to movement in the peripheral vision

- complaining about clothing or shoes

- blurting out thoughts that are either not relevant or not appropriate

- using physical responses rather than verbal ones to convey a message

- failing to raise a hand in class before speaking

- interrupting while people are talking

- saying hurtful things, then feeling sorry later

- having poor anger- and frustration-management skills

- staring off into space

- having difficulty switching tasks

- working hours on one task without getting distracted, even to eat, drink, or go to the restroom

Habituation

Habituation is the getting used to or ignoring of sensory stimuli that are persistent or repetitive, which then frees up attention to focus on things that are important and relevant to the moment. The batter in the baseball game must habituate to the feeling of their tight pants, batting gloves, and batting helmet if they are going to be successful at concentrating on hitting the ball. Too much focus on the sensations of the pants, gloves, or helmet would lead to them feeling uncomfortable and possibly getting distracted by these nonessential messages to the brain.

Common examples of circumstances that children habituate to are feeling the material on the arms from a long-sleeve sweater, feeling the sensation of their shoes on the feet, seeing the harsh light from florescent light bulbs, or hearing background music while studying or concentrating. In normal habituation, the sensation might be noticeable at first, but become less noticeable over time as the brain deems them unimportant.

Children who have difficulty habituating to sensory input are keenly aware of that long-sleeve sweater and often cannot tolerate how it feels on their body. They never stop noticing the shoes on their feet or the harsh light in the classroom, making it impossible to focus on the lesson being taught by the teacher, or they become so focused on the background music that they cannot concentrate on doing their schoolwork. The sensory system never habituates to these common occurrences, leading the child to feel uncomfortable or to behave in ways that are confusing to those around them. Below is a list of behaviors that are common in children who have problems with habituation. Do any of these behaviors sound familiar to your child?

- complaining about how clothing feels on the body

- complaining about noises that other people tune out (like a clock ticking)

- saying they can't focus if there is background noise

- complaining about smells that have been present for a while

Discrimination

Discrimination involves being able to tell the difference between sensory stimuli, such as "Did she say 'eat' or 'beat'?" (auditory), "Is that brown or purple?" (visual), or "Is that a penny or a quarter in my pocket?" (tactile). The baseball player must be able to discriminate between a pitch that is high, low, outside, inside, or right in the strike zone. Otherwise, the batter will swing at every pitch that is thrown. Discrimination helps individuals be successful at playing sports, reading the difference between a *p* and a *q* or a *b* and a *d*, and listening to and following directions. Problems with sensory discrimination cause information to enter the brain as unclear or jumbled, causing children to behave oddly and can make learning terribly difficult. Below is a list of behaviors that are common in children who have problems with discrimination. Do any of these behaviors sound familiar to your child?

- trouble organizing items

- poor skills at matching, even with clothing

- difficulty with reading and comprehension

- problems with math skills due to careless mistakes—for example, by mistaking a 6 for a 9

- difficulty finding items in a cupboard, drawer, in the closet, or on a grocery shelf

- difficulty recognizing, interpreting, or following signs or written directions

- getting lost easily

- difficulty concentrating when there is background noise

- difficulty remembering what people say

- difficulty following directions that include more than two steps at a time

- talking too loud or too soft

- difficulty eating an ice cream cone neatly

- difficulty walking through a room or store without bumping into things

- pushing too hard on objects and accidentally breaking them

- reversing letters or numbers

- difficulty telling time on an analog clock

Children who have problems with sensory regulation may be experiencing problems with either the modulation (accuracy of information) or the correct processing of sensory information (how the information is made sense of)—or both. When your child's nervous system does not function smoothly, due to problems in either of these areas, their behavior or emotions can cause reactions that are confusing and frustrating to you and your child alike.

The Importance of Understanding Sensory Regulation and Dysregulation

Understanding your child's sensory experience helps you make sense of their behavior. Remember, every person has a nervous system, and each nervous system works a little differently. Before making assumptions about emotions and behavior, it is helpful to get some information about what sensory experiences may or may not be contributing to your child's emotions and behaviors. Understanding is the first step in accepting and ultimately changing how you respond to your child and their behavior.

Take a Moment: Take a moment to think about your child and their nervous system. Jot down your thoughts in your journal. What are some sensory triggers that your child reacts to? What sensory experiences are soothing to your child? Do certain environments make reactions better or worse? Do certain times of day change your child's responses? This is very helpful information to have as we approach the second half of this book, as it will guide you toward how to help your child to cope with difficult sensory triggers.

When the nervous system is in a state of being over- or under-stimulated, irrational beliefs, intense emotions, and unusual behavior can occur. Over time, these thoughts, emotions, and reactions can develop into patterns and habits. Sometimes these children are put in therapy and are diagnosed with anxiety disorders, personality disorders, or other behavioral dysfunctions. The children who are described throughout this book have experienced a range of sensory regulation anomalies, sometimes to the point of interfering with their daily functioning in a number of environments (school, home, and social), and may even have been diagnosed with a childhood psychiatric disorder. Sensory regulation problems tend to be on a continuum that results in behavior ranging from simply quirky to downright problematic. Your child may be more in the mild range, while the children described in this book represent the problematic end of the continuum.

Conclusion

In this chapter we examined the functions of the nervous system, including how information is taken in through the near and far senses. You learned how this information is both experienced and processed, as well as what types of behaviors may follow. When a nervous system is functioning normally, this process works well, and the individual is able to maintain a sense of harmony or equilibrium. When the nervous system has problems with the intake, organization, or processing of sensory information, unusual or confusing behaviors can result.

We then looked at the results of what each sense looks like when it is either over-responsive or under-responsive. Behaviors that correspond to each end of the spectrum were outlined and examples of over- and under-responsive reactions to different sensory input were illuminated. We also reviewed three important functions of the nervous system's processing of information: inhibition, habituation, and discrimination. Problems in any of these areas can cause information in the nervous system to become faulty. Faulty information unfortunately leads to intense emotions and problematic behaviors.

Finally, we discussed how these responses can be impacted both positively and negatively by environmental factors such as the time of day, other sensory triggers, and other sensory soothers. Knowing what soothes your child is as important as knowing what exacerbates their nervous system. You should be getting a good idea of how your child's nervous system functions and have some ideas of how they respond to specific sensory triggers.

In the next chapter, we will help you specifically identify your child's sensory triggers and come to a clear understanding of their nervous system. We will describe in detail how problems with regulation impact behavior, as well as how a parent's reactions can contribute to these problems. You are now developing a better understanding of your child and their possible sensory differences, which will help you develop compassion and patience for their behavior. All of this important information is the first step in helping your child successfully cope in a confusing and stimulating world.

CHAPTER 3

When Sensory Regulation Issues
Become a Problem

Chapter 1 focused on the nervous system and how it works in general, outlining how our sensory experience can impact our preferences and our behavior. Chapter 2 outlined what can happen when there are problems in the intake or processing of sensory information. This chapter will focus on (1) identifying specific sensory-based issues in your child and the possible behaviors that they cause, (2) understanding the function of these behaviors, and (3) explaining reinforcement principles, which will illustrate how parents' reactions can unwittingly contribute to behaviors continuing to occur. We hope that in reading this book you will be able to develop a clear path for not only understanding your child's behavior but also creating an effective plan for reducing these challenging behaviors. However, there may be circumstances that warrant consulting with a professional. If the information in this book leads you to believe that your child needs more in-depth evaluation or treatment, we encourage you to consult with a licensed psychologist, psychiatrist, therapist, or occupational therapist. For now, let's take a look at how you can identify possible problems with sensory regulation in your child.

Recognizing Problems with Sensory Regulation

The very fact that you are reading this book suggests that you have suspicions about your child's sensory nervous system, or perhaps a professional has recommended that you read this book to help you understand your child's behavior. To do this, we ask you to first think about your child's early development, before the age of four years old. Ask yourself these questions:

- Was your child colicky and hard to settle as an infant?

- Did your child (and do they still) have difficulty falling asleep?

- Was your child overly responsive to noise? For example, could they be disturbed, startled, or awakened by small noises such as a door closing or light footsteps?

- Was your child under-responsive to noises? For example, could they sleep through loud noises or even seemed to be soothed by them?

- Was your child seemingly oblivious to the happenings in the environment (for example, a dog barking, the phone ringing, buzzing from appliances, etc.)?

- Did your child cry unexpectedly or seemingly for no reason?

- Did your child have comfort items? For example, a favorite blanket that they would not part with, or a pacifier or thumb that was difficult to give up?

- Was your child difficult to toilet train? Did they hold in their stool or urine and have frequent accidents?

- Did your child need certain movement or motion in order to relax? For example, did they have to be driven in the car to fall asleep, held in a rocker, or soothed in a vibrating bouncy chair?

- Did your child react negatively to foods when first introduced?

- Did your child get carsick frequently or become nauseated with movement?

- Would your child eat just about anything, even non-food items?

- Did your child pull their hair out?

- Did your child constantly put things in their mouth to the point where you had to be vigilant about small items or toys that could cause them to choke?

- Did your child do seemingly painful things like bang their head on the wall or floor when frustrated?

- Did your child smell or taste everything that they encountered?

These are just a few common characteristics of young children who may have underlying issues with sensory regulation. In "normal" development, children, especially very young ones, display some or many of these behaviors and grow up with no behavioral problems at all. Usually these sensory reactions are brief events during a developmental stage and disappear rather quickly. Examples of this might be a child who sucks on their shirt collar or picks at mosquito bites for a brief period of time. However, children who have problems with sensory regulation can get "stuck," and these behaviors can persist even though the child has successfully moved to the next stage in development. If you believe that your child had or still has many of these characteristics and continues to struggle with their behavior, you may be on to something important.

Typically, as children age, they become better sensory regulators, and problematic behaviors often disappear. However, not all children follow this path. Some young nervous systems do not develop the ability to tolerate everyday sensations or to self-regulate efficiently or effectively. As a result, these children begin to either avoid sensations that are perceived to be unpleasant (such as refusing to wear tight clothes or socks that have seams, insisting on eating the same foods, or being unwilling to go into a bathroom that has strong smells), or they find alternative ways to achieve a sense of internal calm, like rubbing a blanket, sucking a thumb, or even pulling out hair.

Below is a list of questions that may be helpful in identifying areas that are relevant to your child and their sensory experience now and that will lead to a better understanding of your child's nervous system. By doing so, you will be in a much better position to select ways to increase your child's ability to regulate their nervous system and therefore reduce problem behaviors. In addition, if you were to seek professional help in the future, you will have a detailed description of your child's sensory experience to present to the professional. As you read through the list, make notes in your journal, indicating any areas that you have noticed are problematic. You may begin to identify themes or patterns of emotional and behavioral responses. We have broken the responses down into sensory over-responsive and under-responsive, as well as sensory soothing. You learned in chapter 2 that children who are over-responsive tend to experience certain sensations more profoundly than their peers and, as a result, respond in ways that seem to be an over-reaction to the sensation. Those who are under-responsive experience sensations less profoundly and need more stimulation in order to feel the same sensation. These children seek out sensations and enjoy intense experiences and may turn toward unusual behaviors to soothe their bodies. The under-responders tend to also be the sensory seekers. Think about the range of over- to under-responsive as a continuum, with the middle section being within the "normal" range.

Sensory Over-Responsive

Does your child:

☐ have particular or rigid food preferences?

☐ dislike getting wet?

☐ dislike the beach, particularly the feeling of sand?

☐ dislike messy or yucky-feeling things?

☐ insist on having feet covered or insist on being barefoot?

☐ frequently get motion sick?

☐ prefer bland foods or dislike anything spicy?

☐ become nauseated or gag from certain cooking, cleaning, perfume, or bodily odors?

☐ become upset or overstimulated when people come to the house or when they are in a crowd?

☐ dislike noises that other people are not bothered by (clocks, refrigerators, fans, people talking, blenders, vacuum cleaners, animals, etc.)?

☐ dislike patterns, bright colors, or stripes?

☐ act intolerant of messy environments?

☐ insist that things be placed in a certain order?

☐ dislike food that is touching together on the same plate?

Sensory Under-Responsive

Does your child:

☐ have a hard time recognizing things that most would find alerting or strong?

☐ seem unaware of the smell of foul odors (food that has gone bad, smoke, noxious fumes, or something burning)?

☐ eat anything, even things that other children shy away from (strong flavors, spicy foods, foods that have never been tried before)?

☐ react to pain less intensely than others do?

☐ act lethargic?

☐ have a hard time noticing when hands or face are dirty?

☐ have immediate needs to go to the bathroom?

☐ have frequent accidents with toileting?

☐ have slow reflexes—for example, is slow or unable to catch themselves when falling or protect themselves from getting hurt?

☐ not seem to notice noises that may be bothersome to others?

☐ have trouble waking up in the morning, even with an alarm clock?

☐ bump into things, move in a clumsy fashion, or lack coordination?

Sensory Seeking

Does your child:

☐ enjoy touching things and love to be touched?

☐ constantly fidget with anything and everything?

☐ often touch, twist, or suck on hair (their own or someone else's)?

☐ love fast, spinning, or high rides that may be dangerous?

☐ often rock or sway body back and forth while seated or standing still?

☐ frequently tip their chair back on two legs?

☐ chew on things?

☐ prefer foods with strong tastes and flavors?

☐ bite nails, fingers, lips, or the inside of their cheeks?

☐ love to sleep under heavy blankets?

☐ seek out activities that include a lot of bumping and crashing into things (people or furniture—or both)?

☐ frequently smell unfamiliar objects?

☐ frequently lick or taste objects in the environment that others would not put in their mouth?

Golomb and Mouton-Odum, *Psychological Interventions for Children with Sensory Dysregulation*, Guilford Press, 2016. Reprints with the permission of Guilford Press.

If you find yourself saying yes to many of these items, your child may experience a variety of difficulties with sensory regulation. These problems can affect social, emotional, and behavioral functioning, causing a variety of problems:

- a dislike of changes in plans or routines

- stubborn, defiant, or uncooperative behavior

- emotional and sensitive disposition, being prone to crying

- difficulty finishing tasks and projects

- difficulty making decisions, even simple ones

- a rigid, bossy, and controlling attitude

- a preference for solitary activities over group participation

- an impatient or impulsive nature

- difficulty understanding social cues and nonverbal language

- difficulty obeying people in authority

- difficulty accepting defeat or forgiving oneself

- being frequently angry and easily frustrated

- fearfulness

- panic attacks

- being extremely particular—for example, they can't let certain foods touch each other, or they have to wear certain clothes

- a hatred of surprises

- difficulty making eye contact

Why is all of this important to know? Why does it matter whether your child has issues with sensory regulation or not? The answer is that it can help you understand how your child experiences the sensory world, and, as a result, that understanding will help you make sense of their reactions and behavior. Over time, sensory-based issues can develop into problematic behaviors. Children who have significant difficulties with multiple areas of sensory modulation or processing may experience extreme discomfort throughout childhood and often have problems with inappropriate behavior and regulating their emotions as they mature into adulthood. These children can be calm one minute and then erupt with rage, panic, and frustration, causing their behavior to appear inconsistent or erratic.

Furthermore, these behavioral reactions seem to occur completely out of the blue, appear unrelated to the current situation, and can be perplexing to those around them. When problems with sensory regulation are present, it not only poses a challenge for the child but also profoundly affects those caring for the child, particularly family members, teachers, and siblings. Parents, however, tend to be the people most acutely affected by these behaviors and the people in the best position to help. Managing schedules, daily routines, playdates, and meals; teaching manners; and other day-to-day parent responsibilities can be extremely difficult and enormously frustrating for the parent or caregiver when sensory regulation issues are present. Learning more effective ways to parent a child who struggles with sensory regulation can be game changing. Before getting to the specifics of parenting, let's understand how specific behaviors, even strange ones, serve a function for children in their lives.

Understanding the Function of Behaviors

Recognizing the problems that some children have with sensory regulation helps explain their problematic behaviors, because we can see that they serve a function. These behaviors can be seen as a reaction to some unpleasant sensory experience—the behavior is either a way of avoiding something unpleasant or an attempt to seek out a pleasant sensory experience (avoiding something *bad* or seeking something *good*). For example, when a child refuses to go to the pool with their family, it may be that they are attempting to escape having water splashed in their face. Not going to the pool seems like a reasonable way to achieve comfort (or to avoid discomfort), even if it means inconveniencing the rest of the family. In this way, these behaviors seem more understandable and can be viewed as adaptive or functional for the child.

Another example might be a child who has a reactive arousal system and therefore dislikes surprises. Children such as this develop a strong need for the environment and routine to be predictable and the same every day. This child knows that schedule changes result in extremely uncomfortable feelings—so extreme that the child is not just resistant to change but is actually frightened of how it may make them feel. Parents, teachers, and other caretakers may view extreme reactions or inflexibility as oppositional, controlling, or compulsive when these reactions are actually just an attempt to achieve some level of comfort, and thus serve a function for the child. Understanding the functional nature of your child's behavior can help you be more supportive and less frustrated when your child displays these seemingly irrational behaviors. There are many other examples of common functional responses to sensory stimuli:

- avoidance of loud noises that hurt the ears, such as loud flushing toilets and hand dryers

- avoidance of eating foods that cause strong reactions such as nausea, vomiting, or disgust

- smelling objects in the environment to increase a positive sensation or create awareness

- keeping one's personal space very orderly to avoid visual clutter or chaos

- touching or rubbing objects for soothing

- pulling hair to remove hairs that feel rough or thick because it feels good to rub those hairs between the fingers

- liking loud music played while studying or relaxing

- refusing to go to the bathroom for days, causing leaks or accidents

The above list includes just a few of the many behaviors that often perplex parents and are misidentified as "problems" when they are not fully understood. When evaluating behavior, we seek to understand many aspects of a child's behavior to make sure we approach change with all of the facts. This is referred to as the ABCs of behavior: A—antecedents (what happened right before the behavior was observed), B—the behavior itself (what the child does), and C—consequences or outcomes of the behavior (reduction in a negative state, increase in a positive state, environmental reactions to the behavior, parent attention, or accommodation).

Lucy is six years old and in the first grade at her new public school. She likes school, and in the first few weeks, she has made some friends with whom she feels close. This year her school has increased the frequency of emergency drills to ensure that the faculty, staff, and children are prepared in case of an emergency situation. Lucy, however, has an over-responsive auditory system, and the sound of the alarm frightened her the first time it sounded. She cried, became hysterical, and hugged her teacher throughout the drill. Her mother was called, and Lucy went home from school that day as she was not able to recover from the event of the alarm sounding. She became terrified that the alarm would sound again and was unable to focus on her teacher in the days and weeks after the drill.

When a child such as Lucy has a sensitive auditory system, a loud fire alarm at school (antecedent) may feel painful and elicit the response of screaming and crying (behavior) followed by her having to leave school for the day due to feeling frightened that the sound could happen again (consequence). What is learned from this one experience is complex. First, she learns that fire alarms are painful and unpredictable. Second, she learns to avoid them (she left school as a result of the alarm). Finally, she learns that leaving school provides relief from the fear that the alarm may go off again. In the same way that a dog barks at the postal worker, sensing danger, then feeling relief when the postal worker leaves (after delivering the mail), fear can be learned in response to a misperceived sensory experience (over-responsive to auditory stimuli) and appropriate action is taken (avoidance of school to avoid hearing fire alarms). Over time and without intervention, this fear may spread to other loud noises, such as the sirens of fire engines and ambulances, balloons popping, fireworks, and loud concerts, creating a much more confusing picture. In addition, she may also learn that certain environments don't feel safe and therefore should be avoided—for example, school, Fourth of July celebrations, concerts, or birthday parties, where there may be balloons. Over time, she may avoid a host of common activities, be diagnosed with a phobia or other anxiety disorder, or be seen as oppositional, causing frustration within the family.

Take a Moment: For the next week, make notes in your journal every time your child has an unusual reaction. Note the ABCs of the behavior. First, note the environment: what was the situation when the behavior occurred (place, time of day, day of week, who was present)? Second, note the antecedent: what happened just before the behavior occurred (internal sensory experiences, as well as external triggers, such as noise level, temperature, smell, visual elements, and tactile information)? Third, note the behavior: what was the specific behavior that occurred (shutting down, crying, refusal, avoidance, panic, fear, or anxiety)? Finally, note the consequence: what happened after your child engaged in the behavior (include changes in the child's state of being as well as reactions from those around the child)? Was the unpleasant trigger avoided? Did your child receive a scolding after it? Did your child get to eat something else after refusing to eat? Sometimes it is helpful to keep notes in a table. You can make a table like this one to keep your ABC notes organized.

ABCs of Behavior Chart

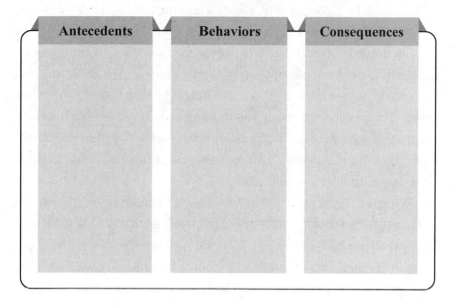

Antecedents	Behaviors	Consequences

Be very specific about sensory aspects of the environment that may have contributed to the behavior (smell, sound, sight, touch, taste, movement, etc.), particularly those you made note of earlier in this chapter. After a week of monitoring, you will begin to notice patterns, common sensory triggers, and behavioral responses to these triggers. You may also notice patterns of how you or others respond to these situations that could inadvertently be encouraging the problem behavior. Information gathered will help you identify sensory-based triggers and accommodating behaviors that will help you, in the second half of this book, identify self-regulation solutions for your child.

As parents, you are not only affected on a daily basis by your child's behaviors, but you are also the people in the best position to help your child manage themselves. While you are not responsible for causing these problems with your child, you are an important part of the solution. How you respond to your child's behavior helps shape and modify that behavior in the future. Going back to the school fire alarm example—if Lucy's parents find out when all fire alarms are going to happen in school, then remove her from school on those days to avoid her having to hear the alarm, they may believe they are helping Lucy by helping her avoid that scary event. In reality, they are potentially supporting Lucy's fear and "teaching" her to avoid scary events in the future.

On the other hand, if her parents respond by getting frustrated, ignoring the fear, and forcing Lucy to attend school and face the fire alarm, that fear may grow and spread to other situations where loud sounds are present. In addition, Lucy may feel misunderstood and invalidated. With continued exposure to the random fire alarms without the skills to manage them, Lucy may eventually develop anxiety at school and even in other loud, unpredictable environments.

What is a parent to do? What is needed is a plan to help children such as Lucy develop the skills necessary to tolerate the sound of the fire alarm, so she does not have to avoid it. Thus, she will learn to face her fear, will conquer her anxiety, and will develop confidence to face other unpleasant situations that involve loud noises. The second half of this book will teach you how to support your child in this way by helping them identify problematic sensory issues and successfully face them by using a variety of effective skills to successfully manage emotions, sensations, and behaviors.

Positive and Negative Reinforcement

As a parent, you are in a unique position to be a significant help to your child. How you respond to their behavior has a profound impact on whether or not you will see that behavior again. Behavior develops through a process called "reinforcement." If a child eats a sandwich, and it tastes delicious, that is called "positive reinforcement"—it encourages them to eat more of that type of sandwich in the future. We say that the behavior is positively reinforced. There is another type of reinforcement that can encourage a behavior that is called "negative reinforcement." Negative reinforcement is when a negative is removed, which creates a positive result. For example, when a child is feeling hungry, and they eat a sandwich, and that feeling of hunger goes away, that is *positive*. By removing a negative (feeling hungry), a positive outcome occurs. Both of these examples are *internal*, meaning that the outcome occurs inside of the person.

So, reinforcement can be *internal positive* or *internal negative*, both of which encourage the behavior to happen again.

External reinforcement can be both positive and negative as well. When a child who is a fussy eater eats a sandwich, and their parent gets really excited and offers them a cookie, that is a *positive external* reinforcement. It encourages the child to eat the sandwich in the future. The behavior is external because the outcome of their behavior is outside of them and involves receiving a reward for the behavior that they perceive to be positive. If, on the other hand, after being teased regularly for picky eating habits, a child eats a sandwich that they wouldn't normally touch, and their peers then stop teasing them, this is *external negative* reinforcement, because the outcome (removing a negative) is outside of their body. This removal of the negative then has a positive impact on the behavior happening again in the future. The Two-by-Two Reinforcement Table below can be helpful in understanding how different reinforcements work. It was developed by John Walkup, MD, a psychiatrist at Northwestern University in Chicago who works with many children with sensory-based disorders.

Two-by-Two Reinforcement Table

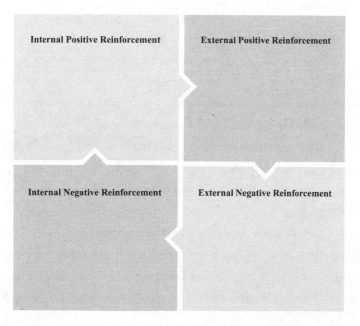

| Internal Positive Reinforcement | External Positive Reinforcement |
| Internal Negative Reinforcement | External Negative Reinforcement |

Parent Accommodation

Sometimes parents, without realizing it, will engage in behaviors that perpetuate their child's unhealthy behavior. Let's look back at the example of Aisha from chapter 2. Aisha could not stand the sound of her mother's chewing at the dinner table. How her parents responded to her angry reaction may play a part in whether or not Aisha will react this way in the future. First, Aisha's dad sent her to her room. In his mind, he was giving a punishment, but in reality he engaged in *negative internal* reinforcement: he removed the negative (allowing her to leave the room so that she no longer had to hear her mother chewing), which gave her relief and therefore was positive. What Aisha learned is that if she yells, she will get to leave the dinner table and not have to hear that awful sound anymore (removal of a negative). Her father also inadvertently engaged in *positive external* reinforcement, because Aisha got to play her video game on her tablet in her room, something she enjoyed doing. Even without thinking about it, Aisha is more likely to yell at her mother the next time she is bothered by her chewing, or maybe even if she is not so bothered by her chewing, simply because she has learned that she will get to leave the dinner table, go to her quiet room, and play her favorite video game.

> **Take a Moment:** Go back to your list of "consequences" from the ABCs of Behavior Chart in the last Take a Moment exercise, earlier in this chapter. Think about how the consequences may have impacted the likelihood of these behaviors happening again. Can you place any of the consequences in the Two-by-Two Reinforcement Table? Is it possible that you are inadvertently encouraging behaviors that you do not want to encourage? Is your child actually benefiting, by either having a negative removed or having a positive added, from the consequence of their behavior? One clue that you may be accommodating the behavior is if the behavior continues. Children typically do not engage in behaviors that do not work for them in some way. For example, if a child has trouble reading in school and feels insecure about their reading ability, they may choose to act up to make other kids in the class laugh to distract them, and the teacher, away from their inability to read well. This child may

have the experience of children laughing and smiling at them, which feels good and encourages more of the silly, disruptive behavior. As a result, the next time this child feels confused in class, they are more likely to act silly to get this response from their teacher and friends. Make a list of all of the possible rein-forcing consequences (both positive and negative) and think about other pos-sible ways to respond to your child in those situations. Be sure to think about other responses that will not inadvertently reinforce their unwanted behavior.

The following is a list of common parental responses that can encour-age child behaviors, even when the parent is trying to do their best to reduce them:

- allowing your child to eat what they want, rather than what is served

- allowing your child to avoid situations that are unpleasant

- giving attention (positive or negative) to behaviors that you do not want to continue

- allowing avoidance of chores or obligations because they are dif-ficult or unpleasant

- not giving consequences when expectations are not met and con-sequences should follow

- walking on eggshells around the child to avoid upsetting them or causing them to react aggressively

- not setting limits on behavior because doing so causes such a reaction from your child

Do you see anything on this list that seems to fit for you and your family? Most families do. These are difficult situations to navigate, par-ticularly when your child has sensory regulation issues. Consider this as a first step in understanding the complex ways your own response will impact your child's behavior. Continue to observe and learn, without changing anything about how you respond, except to develop empathy and awareness. Once you have more information about your child's nervous system and your own reactions, we will explain how you can alter your responses to your child's behavior to have a positive impact on their behavior. For now, just be a good observer of your child's behavior and your response to their behavior. This will allow you to begin to develop a clear understanding of how their behavior and your responses work together.

Providing a Different Perspective

Identifying the presence of sensory regulation problems and how they may relate to problematic behaviors will help you become a good advocate for your child. Knowing that Aisha's auditory system is highly reactive helps us see that her extreme reaction to her mother's chewing is simply an attempt to quiet her nervous system by eliminating the source of discomfort—Mom's chewing. Telling Aisha to get over it or just ignore it or even scolding her may result in her feeling invalidated, frustrated, or helpless, or could result in her refusal to eat at the dinner table. Aisha's angry and avoidant behavior is an attempt to control her discomfort by avoiding the unpleasant noise of her mother's chewing and, in her mind, is the only possible solution to a seemingly insurmountable problem. However, her dad's reaction of sending her to her room—and her mom cooking only her favorite foods—has the opposite effect on her behavior. Her parents want to reduce her screaming behavior, but instead they are encouraging it by allowing her to eat her favorite foods, go to her room, and play her favorite video games. As you can see, given her dad's response, Aisha is actually more likely to continue to scream in this situation.

Based on Jean Ayres's work in the 1970s, we propose using multiple soothing elements while encouraging your child to gradually and systematically experience the unpleasant sensation. This provides a foundation so that the child can effectively work toward being able to tolerate these situations without unusual reactions. In addition, teaching calming thoughts and coping skills can reduce anxiety, change beliefs, and increase relaxation. Finally, making these exercises fun or making it a game helps children engage in this process and move toward success. For Aisha, her parents might:

- allow her to wear earplugs or noise-canceling headphones at the dinner table to reduce the noise of her mother's chewing;

- play her favorite music in the kitchen during dinner to reduce the impact of the chewing noises and also provide some positive auditory input;

- teach her to take several deep breaths, calming her nervous system when it gets activated;

- teach her to say calming thoughts during dinner, such as *I can do this!* and *I have a sensitive nervous system. It's okay—I can work with it*; and,

- verbally praise her success and reward her for staying at the table without screaming by allowing her to have video game time after dinner.

Over time, and with practice, Aisha will learn to tolerate these uncomfortable noises and eventually resume her place at the dinner table without conflict. This comprehensive and creative approach to both understanding and addressing sensory-based problems allows your child to learn to manage their dysregulated nervous system.

Conclusion

In this chapter you have learned to recognize the specific challenges your child faces with respect to the functioning of their nervous system. We gave an extensive list of ways that sensory issues can impact childhood behaviors, helping you identify problematic environments and sensory triggers for their problem behaviors. Next, we reviewed the ABCs of behavior and helped you see the patterns of antecedents, behaviors, and consequences that serve to perpetuate these behaviors through positive and negative reinforcement, both internally and externally. Finally, we reviewed how important your reactions to your child's behavior are. Parent accommodation is a common yet problematic response that can have unintended results on your child's future behavior. In chapter 4, you will be introduced to the ways that problems in the sensory system can look like actual childhood psychological disorders. We will review common childhood diagnoses and explain how problems with sensory regulation can cause symptoms that either mimic or contribute to these disorders. Without proper perspective, children can be misdiagnosed and receive treatment that is not helpful in reducing symptoms.

CHAPTER 4

Sensory Regulation Issues Can Look Like Other Disorders

As you learned in chapter 3, behaviors associated with underlying problems with sensory regulation can be both mystifying and frustrating. In more pronounced cases, children with these issues can appear as having a number of psychiatric disorders, such as obsessive-compulsive disorder, panic disorder, specific phobia, social phobia, generalized anxiety disorder, and oppositional defiant disorder. Other times, sensory sensitivities may lead to a range of difficulties and dysfunction due to disgust and misophonia (a hatred of certain types of noise). This chapter will help you see how common childhood behaviors can be sensory based, but if the sensory origin is not identified, these children can be mistakenly diagnosed as having an anxiety disorder and could get treatment that is not helpful. We are not saying that children do not have these anxiety disorders, nor are we asking you to diagnose your child, but we are saying that if your child looks like they have anxiety as well as difficulty with sensory regulation, you might want to keep reading to further understand their behavior.

Jason, who was described at the beginning of chapter 1, is a good example of a child who might easily get a diagnosis of oppositional defiant disorder, ADHD, or ASD, while the true cause of his behavior is simply his dysregulated nervous system. So keep in mind that if your child has been diagnosed with a psychological disorder *and* they have sensory regulation issues, you may want to seek guidance from a trained professional to help determine whether the sensory issues are either the cause of the behavior (as in the case of Jason) or exacerbating existing behaviors for your child.

How Sensory Dysregulation Can Masquerade as Anxiety

Sensory regulation problems can look very much like an anxiety disorder, and sometimes children are misdiagnosed and mistreated. You may think of your child as obsessive or phobic, when they may actually be reacting to their over- or under-responsive nervous system. Unless we know *why* a behavior is happening, we cannot fully understand it or know how to change it. For example, is a child covering their ears out of fear of a certain noise or because that noise hurts their ears? Is a child refusing to get on the airplane out of fear of the plane crashing or because they are uncomfortable with the sounds and smells on the plane? In each of these examples, how we would help the child looks quite different. Without understanding the *why* of behavior, well-trained and well-intentioned therapists might miss the dysregulation of the nervous system and apply a diagnosis and treatment approach that is inappropriate. Unfortunately, parents also make this mistake by assuming that their child's behavior is the result of either fear or a strong will. Making this mistake can lead to parent reactions that are hurtful and confusing to a child. So, how do you know the *why* of a behavior? We recommend that parents use the approaches of *patience* and *gentle inquiry* with their child to better understand what is underlying the behavior. Patience is just that—being willing to observe, learn, and slowly approach your child to understand their behavior. Gentle inquiry is the simple act of being curious about your child's behavior, without judgment. Gentle inquiry is curious—it is not leading, and it is never demanding.

Patience and Gentle Inquiry are the Keys to Understanding Your Child

You might wonder how you can have a constructive conversation with your child about their behavior. The two most important things to remember are to be patient and to use gentle inquiry. Patience is important because there is a good chance that your child will not be able to immediately give you the answer you are seeking. Getting to the bottom of these behaviors is a process that can take some time. Think about it: Why do you do the things you do? Why do you eat when you are not really that hungry? Why do you stay up late when you know you have to get up early? Behavior can be complicated and hard even for adults to understand, much less children. So be patient and notice patterns of behavior over time.

> **Take a Moment:** Take out your journal and write down some thoughts about the following: Think about a situation or an environment that you do not like—maybe it is a place, maybe it is an event, or maybe it is a person or an object. When you are interacting with this situation, how do you feel? What are the specific things about this situation that you do not like? Are there sensory aspects that make you uncomfortable? If so, what are they? How do these sensory aspects feel to you? How does your body respond to them? What behaviors do you engage in when you are interacting with this situation? Do you ever avoid this situation? Now think about how you would describe this experience to another person: What would you say? How would you describe your internal experience? How would you explain exactly how this situation makes you feel?

Common Disorders and Sensory Causes

The following is a description of several childhood disorders that can have underlying sensory causes, as well as how their parents use *patience* and *gentle inquiry* to gain this understanding.

Obsessive-Compulsive Disorder

People with obsessive-compulsive disorder (OCD) have fearful thoughts or worries (obsessions), followed by repetitive behaviors (compulsions) that serve to reduce their thoughts or worries. Fears typically center around something bad happening to oneself or a loved one, and compulsions involve actions focused on preventing it. For example, if a child has a fear of getting sick, they might engage in repetitive handwashing. Another child might fear accidently leaving the front door unlocked, putting the family at risk, so they check repeatedly each night to ensure that the door is locked. Over time, the fearful thoughts and compulsive behaviors become more and more frequent and evolve into an anxiety-management tool that is short-lived and ineffective. Remember the ABCs of behavior discussed in chapter 3 (*antecedent, behavior,* and *consequence*)? The antecedent for the child who is afraid of getting sick might be that they were in close proximity to a sick person at school, the behavior would be handwashing, and the consequence is that they feel relieved that they will not get sick because their hands are now clean. We can see how this behavior serves a function for the child; it reduces their anxiety about getting sick, whether or not they actually had germs on their hands at all.

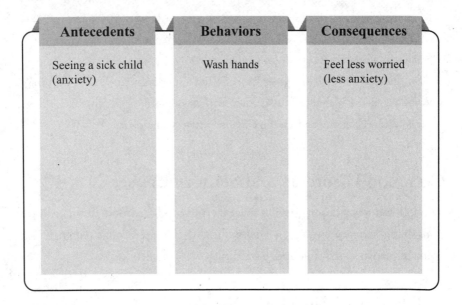

Antecedents	Behaviors	Consequences
Seeing a sick child (anxiety)	Wash hands	Feel less worried (less anxiety)

Children with sensory-based problems can appear in a similar way to children who have OCD. A child might not like the way everyday sensations feel on their fingers and may engage in frequent handwashing to rid themselves of this feeling. In this case, handwashing would not be the result of an obsession or fear, but the result of a touch sensation.

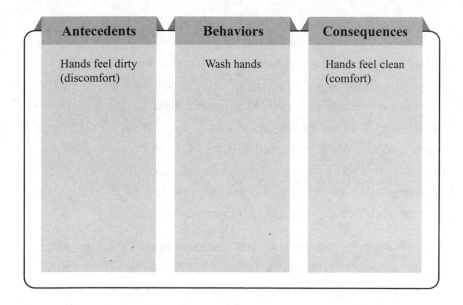

Antecedents	Behaviors	Consequences
Hands feel dirty (discomfort)	Wash hands	Hands feel clean (comfort)

Another child may constantly line up all of their shoes in their closet because they like the way they look when they are perfectly straight. They cannot stand to see even a single shoe out of alignment (visual). This shoe straightening would not be the result of a fear of something bad happening; it would simply be to please their visual sense. You might be able to see how behaviors can be misunderstood by the untrained observer. You may ask, "Why is this important?" The answer is that understanding the *why* leads to very different approaches to helping these children. As we learned in chapter 3, misunderstanding your child's behavior can lead to frustration for parents or even accommodation (inadvertently making the behavior increase). A misdiagnosis can lead to treatments or interventions that are not helpful and, in some cases, may make the problem worse.

How do you, as a parent, know what is actually going on with your child who may look like they have OCD? The first clue that a child may have something other than OCD lies in how one would answer this question: "What would happen if you were not able to perform your repetitive behavior?" For someone who has OCD, the answer is usually a fear of something catastrophic happening—someone would get sick, someone might die, someone's safety could be compromised, and so on. When a child is experiencing sensory issues, the answers to this question tend to be different, lacking any stated fear of a catastrophic result: "Nothing would happen" or "It just wouldn't *feel* right." Usually, the response has to do with some sensory irritation: "I don't like the way the salt and grease from the French fries feels on my fingers, so I have to wash my hands." Because there is no underlying fear, and the source of the discomfort is sensory, we categorize this phenomenon as sensory dysregulation, not OCD.

Here is another example of a child who might look like he has OCD but really has difficulty regulating his nervous system.

Carl is an eleven-year-old boy who is very particular about how things are arranged. As a result, his pediatrician referred him to be evaluated for possible OCD. Carl has to have things "just so"—his pencils need to be lined up evenly and arranged by color; his pillows on his bed have to be fluffed and positioned a certain way; his clothes are hung by color, category, and length; and he has to have his desk clear of all clutter for him to study or do his homework. Carl's mom is quite knowledgeable about sensory issues and has experience with occupational therapy with her older daughter. Carl's mom is patient and observes Carl for a while to see what behaviors he engages in and when. Then, she uses gentle inquiry to try to understand the why of his ordering behavior. "Carl, what do you imagine will happen if you do not line up your pencils exactly right?" His response was: "I don't think anything will happen; I just won't feel right." She delves a little deeper: "What will happen if you don't feel right?" His response intrigues her: "Well, I can't do anything until I line up my pencils just right. I feel terrible, and I just don't like the way it feels." To determine whether it is a sensory-based discomfort rather than a fear-based discomfort, she finally asks: "I wonder if this nervous feeling has anything to do with the way the pencils look to you when they are messy. Do you ever feel like when you look at things that just don't look right to you, you have to fix them?" His response helps her understand the why of his behavior: "Yes, they look messed up and like

*they need to be in order. I have the same feeling when I look at other
things. In my room, I like to make sure the papers on my desk are
straight and the pillows on the bed are even. It just looks so weird to
me when they are not straight. Sometimes I even straighten a picture
on a wall if it is crooked, but I usually do this when no one is looking,
because I don't want anyone to think I am strange." Carl's mom
suspected that poor sensory regulation (visual) might be driving his odd
behavior, so she sought out a therapist who had experience in sensory-
based issues, rather than OCD.*

Seeing his environment lined up and ordered is soothing to Carl's
nervous system, while looking at messed-up pencils, pillows, and clothing
agitates his visual system. Over time, Carl has learned that straightening
things in his environment settles him down, even though he likely cannot
even verbalize this. Unfortunately, this straightening behavior is disruptive to smooth transitions, interferes with his ability to accomplish tasks in
a timely fashion, and can result in Carl having an emotional outburst if
pencils or other items in his environment don't look "just right." The need
to achieve these "just right" feelings or other reactions to sensory experiences can result in many behaviors that look compulsive.

There are a number of behaviors that can be sensory based and may
be mistaken for OCD behaviors, along with the kind of sensory issue each
item is:

- lining items up so that they look right (visual)

- ordering or arranging items so that colors are grouped together
  (visual)

- having to wear certain clothes due to how they look, such as color,
  solid, prints, or patterns (visual)

- needing items such as sheets, blankets, or towels to look a certain
  way in order to use them—this can include lacking dirt (not due
  to worry about dirt or germs), folded a certain way, or in a specific
  place (visual)

- avoiding places or things due to how they smell (olfactory)

- having to wear (or refusing to wear) certain clothes due to how they feel—for example, itchy, scratchy, soft, too tight, too loose (touch)

- avoiding touching certain objects or handwashing in response to hands feeling dirty or sticky, but not due to germs or contamination (touch)

- avoiding foods or drinks due to taste aversions (taste)

- avoiding (or needing) certain auditory stimuli (hearing)

- having to repeat behaviors until they feel right, though not due to superstitious beliefs (interoceptive)

- avoiding going to the bathroom because of unpleasant sensations while voiding (interoceptive)

- compulsive eating behaviors due to not sensing when the stomach is full or hungry (interoceptive)

- compulsive jumping, spinning, or cartwheeling behaviors to achieve a feeling (vestibular)

- compulsive avoidance of activities that involve jumping, spinning, or cartwheeling to avoid feeling uncomfortable (vestibular)

- preoccupation with risk-taking behaviors that feel exciting (vestibular)

- tapping, rubbing, evening up that is not due to superstitious beliefs (proprioceptive)

The key to spotting the difference between a child with OCD and one with underlying problems with sensory regulation is to identify whether or not there is an actual fear present. If no worry seems to be present, you would then want to know whether the worrisome behavior is occurring because the child is trying to manage a difficult sensation. Understanding the origin of your child's behavior will help determine how to best help your child. When your child is struggling with nervous system issues, learning ways to soothe the nervous system can be extremely helpful. If, however, your child is experiencing symptoms of OCD and has concerns about bad things happening if they are not able to engage in the repetitive behavior, working with a trained professional is the best approach. When OCD is not present, parents can often create their own plan that shows compassion toward the challenges of having sensory sensitivities or needs, while at the same time helping their child use effective tools to master the situation. First, however, you must understand the ABCs (antecedents, behavior, consequences) of your child's behaviors.

Here are two examples of children who were struggling with symptoms that at first appeared to be OCD. Each child exhibited an exaggerated or unusual response to sensory experiences, but lacked a feared or catastrophic outcome. Reading these examples will help you learn to recognize your own child's ABCs.

Tyler, a nine-year-old boy, was brought to therapy by his parents who were told by a psychiatrist that he had OCD. Tyler hopped into the office on one foot. He would only hop, rather than walk, from place to place. Instead of sitting down on the couch or a chair, Tyler squatted on the floor, again with only one foot touching the floor. His parents were at wit's end with Tyler's strange obsession with hopping and balancing. The therapist patiently asked Tyler about the hopping and balancing. After a series of gentle inquiries, Tyler stated that he cannot stand the way it feels for both feet to touch the floor at the same time. Even worse is when his bottom is on a chair and his feet touch the floor—it is simply too much touching at one time. He learned that by allowing only one foot to touch at a time, he could reduce this unpleasant feeling and be somewhat comfortable.

Lilly, a six-year-old girl, was diagnosed with OCD by her pediatrician, who was concerned about her washing behaviors. She had a history of handwashing that had really increased when she started first grade. Lilly frequently asked to leave class to go to the bathroom to wash and was known to wash up to forty times a day. Lilly's parents were worried. Lilly's hands were so dry and chapped from all the washing that they had removed the soap from bathrooms around the house. Most recently, she had begun to refuse to put her underwear back on after using the restroom, because she felt as if urine might have gotten on her underwear. Her parents were confused and did not know how to handle this difficult situation, especially at school. When asked gently about her washing, Lilly stated that she does not like the way her hands feel when she has touched certain things, like playdough or glue. Her hands feel sticky or like there is a film on them, even if there is no residue on her hands.

After talking with a family friend who was an occupational therapist, Lilly's mom was patient and, after observing the types of things that Lilly tended to react to, she decided to try an experiment. She and Lilly touched a number of objects at home, including playdough. Lilly became focused on washing her hands very soon after touching the playdough. Using gentle inquiry, her mom asked her what she thinks would happen if she were not able to wash her hands. Lilly stated, "I am not scared of dirt or germs, I just do not like the way my hands feel after touching the sticky playdough. They feel yucky." When asked about using the restroom and changing her underwear, Lilly stated that she cannot stand the way it feels when even a drop of urine gets onto her underwear. She denied that the feeling had to do with contamination or the urine itself, it just feels terribly uncomfortable when the cold wetness touches her body. In an attempt to reduce the chances of her getting urine in her underwear, she would wipe for minutes at a time, leading to sore and chapped skin.

Both of these examples highlight how sensory sensitivities can easily be mistaken for symptoms of OCD. The other end of the responsiveness spectrum can also look like OCD. When a child is seeking stimulation by touching, smelling, licking, or tasting objects, parents and therapists can mistake it for signs of OCD and pursue a course of treatment that will not address the true source of the problem. Again, a thorough evaluation of the nervous system and what sensations a child is seeking, and *why* they are seeking them, can lead to helpful answers. Here is an example of a child who is seeking sensory input but could be mistakenly identified as having OCD.

> *Chase is a ten-year-old boy who started engaging in some strange behaviors that were confusing to his parents. He would deliberately step on cracks in the sidewalk or on the lines of grout between tiles on the floor in a certain way, oftentimes making him look quite strange while he walked. If he touched something with his left hand, he would have to "even up" by immediately touching the same thing with his right. His parents were convinced that he had OCD and had made plans to take him to a therapist who treats OCD. Prior to the appointment, however, his dad remembered that he had experienced some similar behaviors as a child, so he attempted to better understand his son. Using patience and gentle inquiry, he started the conversation by saying, "Chase, I think I might know how you feel when you walk on the sidewalk. I am curious what it feels like to you when you have to step on the cracks the way you do." Chase responded by saying, "I can feel a tingling in my foot, telling me that I have to step on the cracks. It is like my foot is telling me exactly where to step to make the feeling go away." His father probed on, "So what would happen if you did not step on the cracks like that? How would that feel?" Chase explained, "I am not sure. I have never let it go that long, but I think it would keep feeling weird until I stepped on the crack. It is the same with my hands; if I touch the sofa with one hand, my other hand starts tingling, telling me that I need to touch the sofa with that hand as well. It tingles until I touch with it, then the tingling stops right away."*

Again, it is the sensory nervous system that is driving Chase's behavior, not a fear that something bad will happen if he does not perform the action. When sensory dysregulation is not recognized, families oftentimes spend unnecessary time, energy, and effort in search of treatment that is not likely to be effective.

Panic Disorder

Panic disorder is described as a sudden onset of high anxiety accompanied by a variety of physical symptoms (dizziness, light-headedness, a rapid heartbeat, sweating, and shallow breath, to name a few). In addition, the person often fears that they will lose control of themselves (such as by fainting), that they will have a heart attack, or even that they might die. Panic attacks are frequently triggered in environments where a child feels like they are trapped and cannot easily get out, such as standing in a line at a store, navigating a crowded mall, or sitting in the middle of a row in an auditorium or on an airplane. Let's see how *gentle inquiry* can help tease out some sensory regulation issues from true panic symptoms.

Ethan is an eight-year-old boy who has frequent "panic attacks." He explained it to his mother like this: "Sometimes I just freak out. I have to leave and go home, or I will completely lose it. If you don't want to leave, I will cry and throw a fit until you do. I just can't stand it when that happens." His mother gently asked him, "Tell me about what it feels like right before you have the 'freak out.'" Ethan responded, "Well, usually I am in a situation that is crowded and loud, with lots of people." She then asked, "What about the situation do you not like? What are you thinking about when you are in that situation, with lots of people and noise?" He answered, "I am thinking that I need to get out. I just can't stand all of the noise and the smell of the people, and I hate it when they are bumping into me or brushing against me, and all of the noise won't stop. It is just awful! The only thing I can think about is being home and in my room, where it is quiet and where I can lie on my bed and feel my soft blankets and calm down." His mother finally understood and stated, "Ethan, please let me know when you are starting to feel this way so I can help you find a place to escape all of the people and the noise." Ethan agreed, "Thanks, Mom, that would be great!"

Sensory processes seem to be underlying Ethan's discomfort, rather than a panic disorder. He gets overstimulated in environments that have lots of noise, smells, touch, and visual input, causing him to feel overloaded and to want to leave immediately. Instead of recognizing that he does not like these environments, his body goes into a flight response and he feels the need to leave immediately. For Ethan, he may not have any idea about why these episodes occur, thinking that they are random. Helping him understand his nervous system and what it can and cannot handle will make him feel more in control over his responses, and knowing when he may be triggered will help him recognize when he should leave a situation before he gets too stimulated. While his behavior might appear to be a panic attack, it is really a response to a sensory dysfunction that can be addressed in a much different way than a traditional panic attack.

Specific Phobias

Specific phobias are somewhat common in children and include intense and disabling fears of things like dogs, cats, insects, loud sounds, vomit, and specific experiences, such as roller coasters, riding a bicycle, long car trips, and a host of other stimuli. Parents usually become concerned when their child becomes anxious around these triggers or avoids them altogether. When there is a history of a scary event for the child— for example, being frightened by a dog   a phobia may develop. However, if there is no memory of a traumatic experience (that is, if the child never had a scary encounter with a dog or witnessed another person being bitten or snarled at by an angry dog), then asking targeted questions about their sensory experience is worth pursuing. The following is an example of a child describing what might look like a fear of dogs.

Isabel is a ten-year-old who refuses to be around dogs of any kind. She responds to dogs with what looks like fear—she runs away from any dog she sees, refuses to get out of the car at the park if a dog is present, will not enter a home where there is a dog, and asks copious questions about potential dog situations before going someplace. Isabel explained it this way: "I do not want to even see a dog or go into someone's house that has a dog. I just do not like them." When her mom gently inquired about past times when she was around dogs, she responded, "A few years ago I used to go to my friend Sasha's house, and her dog was smelly. He would put his wet nose on me and lick my hand and leg. I hate it when they get their wet tongue on me. I cannot stand the way they smell and lick you all the time. People say that dogs are soft, and they call the licks 'kisses,' but I think that their hair is wiry, I don't want to feel their tongue, and I hate to have their slobber on my hands or their cold nose on my skin. I just scream and run if I see one so I don't have to smell or touch it, and it won't touch me."

This is an example of a phobic-like reaction to sensory-based concerns (smell, touch). There are many other common experiences that can elicit a response such as anxious avoidance or panic reactions:

- loud flushing toilets, leading to avoidance of restrooms or refusing to flush toilets (auditory)

- loud hand dryers, resulting in avoidance of public restrooms (auditory)

- the noise of fireworks, leading to avoidance of any type of celebration where they may be present (auditory)

- balloons popping, eliciting avoidance of birthday parties (auditory)

- certain animals, causing avoidance of going to houses, parks, or public places where these animals might be present (auditory, touch, smell)

- places with strong odors such public restrooms, stables, portable latrines, and certain restaurants, leading to aversions to these places (smell)

- dirty dishes after a meal, with smells and sights of the mixed remains of the food still on the plates, leading to a refusal to help wash the dishes (visual, olfactory)

- amusement parks and rides (can be due to vestibular experiences, sounds, smells, visual stimulation, or some combination of all)

- long car rides, leading to avoidance of family vacations, visiting relatives or friends, or going anywhere that requires a car ride that lasts more than twenty minutes (vestibular)

- eating certain foods (taste, texture, smell)

- clothing (specific types of clothes: socks, shoes, pants, belts, dresses, turtlenecks, high-waisted pants; or certain attributes of clothes: tight, patterned, bright), leading to refusal to wear certain clothes, even if they are incongruent with the environmental demands (for example, wearing athletic shorts to church or wearing shorts when there is snow on the ground) (visual, touch)

Antonio, a seven-year-old boy, was referred to treatment by his pediatrician for a phobia of hand dryers. He stopped traveling with his parents anywhere that would require a rest stop on the way. In addition, Antonio refused to go to restaurants with his family because the restroom might have a hand dryer. When discussing his aversion to hand dryers, Antonio described the loud noise that they made as being extremely uncomfortable and would result with him screaming and running out of the restroom, retreating back to the car, or crying while refusing to finish his dinner. Antonio's mother was able to convince him to accompany the family to a restaurant only if she agreed to go with him into the restroom and guard the hand dryer, so that it would not be used while he was in the bathroom.

It is important to understand why your child may be having a reaction in a specific situation. All too often, parents presume that the nature of the reaction is fear, because it looks a lot like fear; however, this is not always the case. Gentle inquiry and patience with your child are essential when getting the answers you will need to better understand your child's behavior.

Social Phobia

Social phobia is defined as a fear of doing something embarrassing and being judged negatively by others, leading to extreme anxiety and avoidance of social situations, such as public speaking, being in crowds, or going to parties where few people are known. Sometimes, however, fear of social environments is not entirely the result of concerns about negative evaluation. For many children with sensory regulation issues, going to public places is scary (because they don't know what to expect in terms of sights, sounds, smells, and touch), physically uncomfortable (due to unpleasant sights, sounds, smells, tastes, movement, and lots of touch), and unpredictable (the same environment can be different on different days). This avoidance or resistance can look like social anxiety, and it takes a skilled person to decipher what is really going on.

Remember Jose from the book's introduction, who had difficulty with sleepovers due to the overstimulation caused by a combination of sounds, smells, and a lack of sleep? He misinterpreted social interactions with his friends due to sensory difficulties. Eventually, Jose began to avoid social relationships in general. Because of his behavior, he might be considered socially anxious, and without proper treatment, he may eventually develop a bona fide social anxiety disorder. However, understanding the sensory aspects of his behavior would greatly help his parents support him and guide him in these difficult sensory situations. Further, parental support helps children develop better coping skills, thus reducing problematic behavior, and it can prevent other problems from developing in the future.

Kiera is a thirteen-year-old in the seventh grade. She has always preferred small groups of friends and has avoided gatherings where more than two or three people would be present. She had been avoiding birthday parties, the circus, and outings with large groups for years, but it was now becoming a problem, as she was being invited to amusement parks, skating rinks, movies, and other venues that she wanted to visit with her friends. Not wanting to assume that Kiera did not like other girls her age, her dad used gentle inquiry to better understand her avoidance. He asked, "Kiera, I am curious about why you don't want to go to the birthday party at the skating rink. Is there something that makes you not want to go?" Kiera responded that she really wants to go to the party, but that she cannot stand the feeling of people touching her in a crowd, the noise, the visual stimulation of so many people together, the smells of all of the people, and the overall chaos of the event. Once they knew the origin of her discomfort, her parents were able to seek the interventions she needed so that she could go to the skating party, rather than allowing her to miss out on events that she would like to enjoy.

Another way that sensory issues can affect social relationships involves eye contact. Children with visual sensitivities often avoid making eye contact, as the visual stimulation of making eye contact can be too overwhelming. Much social learning takes place during conversations while a person is looking at another person—reading their expression and noticing subtle changes in their face and body language. Children who avoid making eye contact may miss out on years of social learning. The result may be lower social confidence, difficulty reading social situations, inappropriate social responses, and overall social incompetence. Parents may become frustrated with a child who does not make eye contact, thinking that the behavior is disrespectful or rude. Understandably, parents may try to help by frequently reminding their child to make good eye contact, often in the presence of the person they are speaking with. Unfortunately, these comments can be embarrassing and feel invalidating for children with sensory issues, adding to their social discomfort. If gentle inquiry with your child results in their telling you that they feel overwhelmed by looking into another person's eyes, you can suggest techniques such as looking at their eyebrows or their forehead, instead of their eyes, so that the person thinks that they are making eye contact.

Generalized Anxiety Disorder

Generalized anxiety disorder (GAD) is essentially a worry disorder. People with GAD worry about a wide variety of things (What should I wear? What will happen? Will things go well? Will I fail? Is everything okay?). GAD worry does not have a specific theme (unlike the case with OCD, where people typically worry about the same sort of thing, like contamination), and the worrying takes up a significant amount of a person's time and energy, even to the point that it interferes in their life and functioning. When a child has a dysregulated nervous system, it can look like this type of worry.

> Ling is a nine-year-old in the fourth grade. She does well in school and plays sports. Ling is constantly asking her parents questions. For example, on a Friday night after her soccer game, her family was planning to go out to eat on the way home. When told that they would stop for dinner, the questions began: "Where are we going for dinner? Who will be there? Have we been there before? What kind of food do they have? Will I like it? Will it be crowded? What are the bathrooms like? Do they play music there? Do they serve dessert?" Ling's parents were exhausted by the time they got to the restaurant. If they did not know the answer to her questions, she became upset and asked it they could please go to a restaurant that she was familiar with. Ling's father took some time to talk to Ling about why she wanted to know all of these things, and Ling was able to explain that she wanted to be ready if there were things she did not like, such as if the restaurant was very loud, crowded, served strange foods, or had smelly bathrooms. By asking questions, she was trying to get important information about the environment at the restaurant to help her know what to expect. Ling would prefer to always go to the same restaurant and eat the same food, so she would know that there would be no surprises.

Ling is a good example of a child with a sensitive nervous system who is trying to manage her senses by knowing her environment and what to expect. After her parents patiently asked her questions to help understand the nature of her questions, they were able to calm down and respond with less frustration. Her dad made up a story about "Ling the Adventurer," who would seek out new experiences every day and explore new places on her travels. From then on, when the family went to new places, Ling and her parents would talk about what that adventure might be like for each of them, acknowledging that none of them knew for sure what the adventure would be like. After a visit to a new place, they would talk about the adventure, discussing what each of them liked, as well as what they did not like about the place from a sensory perspective.

Oppositional Defiant Disorder

Oppositional defiant disorder (ODD) is characterized by a pattern of behavior that appears oppositional. Children with ODD often have irritable moods, behavioral outbursts, and argumentative or defiant behaviors, even about seemingly easy things to do. When a child has sensory regulation issues, they will get upset, refuse to participate, or flat out throw a fit when facing experiences that physically feel intolerable. Think about it—if you were told that you were going to eat a picnic at the park while sitting on an anthill, you might experience some resistance to the picnic. There are many examples of oppositional behaviors that also can be sensory based:

- the child is rigid about change (has a hard time with transitions)

- the child is described as stubborn, uncooperative, or defiant

- the child is highly reactive and cries easily

- the child refuses to do things and cannot explain why

- the child runs away from situations

- the child has difficulty making decisions

- the child can be seen as bossy and controlling

- the child frequently gets angry or has moments of rage

- the child hates surprises

- the child may avoid eye contact

- the child has trouble relating to and socializing with peers

It is important to understand what is actually going on with your child—whether the behavior is truly defiant or simply an attempt to avoid unpleasant sensory experiences.

Anders is a nine-year-old who has been getting into trouble at school for refusing to cooperate with the rules of the classroom and cafeteria. He refuses to sit at his desk and will not stand in line for lunch in the cafeteria. The curious principal asked him what was going on with not sitting in his seat. He replied, "The seat is really cold in the morning. It is so cold that I feel like it is freezing my butt and legs! Also, after lunch the seat in my other room is really scratchy and I can't stand how it feels on my legs. I prefer to stand and not sit down." "How about the lunch line—why don't you like to get in line?" she asked him. He responded, "I hate it when the other kids touch me. It feels like I am being attacked when I stand in line, so I just stand out of line to avoid getting touched. If they want to send me to suspension for that, I guess I will just have to go."

Although on the surface Anders looks as if he is oppositional and defiant, he is actually just trying to stay comfortable in his body. Not only was this information integral to helping him navigate the school environment successfully, but it also helped the principal support him and advocate for him in the classroom. The principal spoke to his teacher, and they decided to allow Anders to bring a pillow to school to sit on to reduce the cold and itchy feelings. He was also allowed to stand out of line at lunch to reduce the amount of touching that he had to endure. Helping your child understand how their nervous system functions and how to effectively manage the many internal and external sensory experiences is really important. This simple act could help change the trajectory of your child's life and can help them be a better regulator of their nervous system.

Disgust

Disgust is an interesting and important topic when discussing the sensory system. Like many sensory issues, disgust may weave itself through a wide range of issues and can often be misunderstood. Disgust is defined as a strong feeling of dislike for something that has an unpleasant appearance, taste, or smell. By definition, disgust is sensory based. When children have issues with sensory regulation, this strong feeling of dislike may look like anxiety, avoidance, refusal, or anger.

An important area where disgust is a primary focus of treatment is with fear of vomit or vomiting (emetophobia). Many times these children can be misdiagnosed as having an eating disorder (limiting food intake to avoid the possibility of vomiting), problems with refusing to go to school (fear of getting sick or seeing someone else vomit), social anxiety (fear of vomiting or seeing someone vomit in public), or a specific phobia (fear of seeing vomit or someone vomiting). However, disgust is not limited to fear of vomit. Many children find certain activities to be disgusting—emptying the trash, cleaning the dishes, scrubbing the toilet (not due to contamination fears), cleaning up after a dog, or managing their own toileting needs—and this may result in anxious, avoidant behavior. In addition to activities, other things can be considered disgusting as well, including roaches, spiders, certain animals (rats, frogs, or lizards), certain foods, trash, blood, urine, feces, objects with specific textures, genitals, and irregularities of any kind (skin eruptions, scabs, warts, etc.), which may result in phobic-like responses. Most of us would likely all agree that many of those things are indeed disgusting—or at least seriously unpleasant. However, most people can experience disgust without feeling anxious. For children with sensory regulation issues, disgust can trigger the sympathetic nervous system's fight-flight-or-freeze response and results in intense fear-like reactions. Eventually, children mistake disgust for anxiety and respond accordingly, with avoidance or refusal. Here is an example of what might be mistaken for oppositional behavior, which really stems from feelings of disgust:

> Ingrid, aged ten years, did not like to complete all of her chores. Her parents were frustrated with her seemingly defiant behavior and had been punishing her for not completing her responsibilities. When asked more specifically about why she failed to complete certain chores, she responded: "Actually I do most of my chores. I just don't like doing the dishes. I cannot stand to see all of the food mashed together. When it mixes with water, and the whole disgusting mess goes down the sink, it makes me want to throw up. I literally gag when I see it. It's not just the way it looks. It's also how it smells, how it feels, the whole experience is totally disgusting. I will do just about any chore as long as I don't have to do the dishes!"

Again, the question of the *why*—as well as being patient and using gentle inquiry—can be immensely helpful in completely understanding what is driving your child's behavior, which makes it much easier to respond in a compassionate way.

Misophonia

Misophonia is defined as a hatred of specific sounds, causing a person to react with anger or extreme frustration and frequently involves disgust. The sound of a person chewing food is often a trigger for a person with misophonia and can be perceived to be disgusting, as seen in the example of Aisha from chapter 3, who was asked to leave the dinner table when she yelled at her mother for chewing loudly. Other sounds, such as crumpling paper, clicking a pen, or tapping fingers can elicit this rage reaction and can be misunderstood as a variety of behavioral disorders. Misophonia is a sensory system regulation issue that results in extreme anger and can be quite perplexing for parents, teachers, and other children.

Conclusion

In this chapter, we have given examples of numerous children who appear to have childhood disorders but actually have sensory-based problems. As stated earlier in this chapter, the key to understanding behavior is knowing the *why* of the behavior. Patience is one of the keys to success in getting to the bottom of your child's behavior, and gentle inquiry is the other. Gentle inquiry is a way of asking questions that does not feel like an interrogation. When you are talking with your child about their experience, it is important to be curious, but not demanding. Use phrases like "I wonder how that feels to your fingers?" and "I am curious about how your body feels when all of those people are bumping into you in the crowd?" Know that your child might respond with "I have no idea." Let that be okay, and maybe wait until another time to approach the conversation again. They might simply not know how to explain how they feel, but your gentle questions might cause them to think about it, and they might be able to answer you in the future.

Using your own personal experience can be helpful in normalizing the situation for your child. Sharing how specific sensory experiences impact you and wondering how they impact your child can help open the door for further exploration. For example, with regard to Isabel, who was diagnosed with a fear of dogs, her mother was able to use gentle inquiry to help identify what was driving her avoidance of dogs: "Isabel, I have noticed that you do not like to be around dogs. I am curious about this, as you are such an animal lover and are so sweet to animals. I wonder why you do not like dogs?" You may recall that Isabel responded that she did not like the way they smell, feel, and how they lick her skin. Her mom then shared, "That reminds me of when I was a girl, and I did not like going to farms because of the way the farm animals smell, especially in the barn. My grandparents had a farm with many horses, cows, and goats, and I did not like going to visit them, just because of this." Isabel was then more comfortable opening up to her mother about her own sensory experience, feeling like her mother not only understood her but was also on her team.

In this chapter we have taken the information from chapters 1 to 3, explaining how the nervous system works and how it works when a child is over- or under-responsive, and given specific examples of how behavioral responses to sensory information can masquerade as a variety of childhood psychological disorders. We explained why understanding what is driving the behavior is the key to knowing how to manage it. Finally, we have given you tools to help you glean this information from your child in a loving and supportive way—patience and gentle inquiry.

By now you should have a pretty good idea about your child's nervous system: what they like and dislike, how they are over- or under-responsive, how they respond when put in situations that are unpleasant to their senses, and how their behavioral responses might look like one or more psychological disorders. In the next chapter, we will discuss different childhood disorders that have common sensory aspects in addition to the disorder. Whereas in this chapter we talked about how sensory system issues can look like a specific childhood disorder, the next chapter will look at disorders that frequently occur alongside problems in the sensory system. Addressing the sensory system in these cases can help reduce the co-occurring disorder.

CHAPTER 5

Difficulty with Sensory Regulation Is Common in Conjunction with Several Childhood Disorders

While in chapter 4 we discussed how problems in the sensory system can actually look like a childhood disorder, this chapter will discuss common childhood disorders that are often accompanied by sensory regulation problems. Why is this important to talk about? Because if your child is diagnosed with one of these disorders, you will want to take a good look at their sensory functioning and then focus on helping your child take better care of their sensory system. Helping to soothe the sensory system often reduces the symptoms of the other disorder. For example, children who pull out their hair have a variety of sensory-based issues. We have seen clinically that helping to soothe the sensory system dramatically reduces hairpulling in children. In addition, children with autism spectrum disorder (ASD), persistent tic disorders (PTDs), and attention deficit hyperactivity disorder (ADHD) also often have sensory issues. This is why it is critical to understand and address any difficulties with sensory regulation, so that you will be better able to help your child function to the best of their ability. This chapter will review and discuss several disorders that have a high rate of sensory regulation issues. The tools of patience and gentle inquiry are helpful when talking to your child about their feelings, behaviors, and responses to sensory experiences. As you learned in the last chapter, understanding *why* a child engages in a behavior is always helpful for understanding the behavior itself. In addition, with children in these specific categories, it also allows you to help your child self-regulate, possibly reducing other unwanted behaviors.

Body-Focused Repetitive Behaviors

Body-focused repetitive behaviors (BFRBs) include repetitive hairpulling (trichotillomania), skin picking (excoriation disorder), nail biting, nail picking, cuticle biting or picking, biting the inside of the cheek, and lip biting. For many children with BFRBs, sensory regulation difficulties are the cornerstone of the problematic behavior. Children who pull and pick often do so to increase a pleasurable sensation or to reduce an unwanted sensory experience. There are many kinds of sensory-based pulling and picking behaviors:

- pulling hair that looks different (thin, thick, curly, dark, white) (visual)

- pulling hair that looks out of place (visual)

- pulling hair that feels different (coarse, fine, sharp, thick) (tactile)

- pulling to look at or feel the hair or hair bulb that is cool and wet (tactile, visual)

- pulling hair to rub the hair or hair bulb along the face or lips (tactile, taste)

- pulling hair to nibble the hair or hair bulb or to eat the hair or hair bulb (taste)

- pulling hair to smell the hair or hair bulb (olfactory)

- pulling hair to hear the eyelid slap on the eyeball (auditory)

- picking the skin to eliminate a scab or blemish or to change the way it looks (tactile, visual)

- picking the nail to smooth out the rough edge (tactile)

- picking the skin to eliminate a scab or blemish or to change the way it feels—for example, to make it smooth (tactile)

- picking skin (something like a pimple or a scab) to see the liquid underneath the skin come out (visual)

- picking skin to smell the liquid underneath the skin (olfactory)

- picking skin to eat the skin, scab, or liquid underneath the skin (taste)

- picking skin to reduce the feeling of a bump, hangnail, or loose skin on the lip or cheek (tactile)

- biting the inside of the cheek to remove a bump or rough spot (tactile)

- biting the lip to remove rough or dead skin (tactile)

- picking the skin around the fingernail or toenail to remove loose or dead skin (tactile, visual)

Pulling and picking behaviors are also described by sufferers as meeting a deeper neurological need as well. People describe BFRBs as relaxing, calming, a tension-reducing behavior, or even stimulating and energizing, suggesting that BFRBs impact the arousal and calming systems. Overlooking this important sensory piece may make attempts to help your child successfully manage their behavior ineffective, causing frustration for both you and your child. For many people with a BFRB, the entire reason for engaging in the behavior is to achieve a certain sensory experience.

Caitlin is a twelve-year-old girl who started pulling out her hair a few months ago. She pulled out all of her eyelashes and eyebrows, and her parents were shocked. They immediately brought her to therapy to find out what was wrong with her and how to get her to stop this disfiguring behavior. When patiently gathering information about the behavior, her therapist used gentle inquiry to learn that Caitlin initially started pulling her pubic hair due to the dark appearance of the new, unusual hair. As new pubic hairs appeared, she pulled them out right away, because they were coarser and darker than her other hair, and it looked and felt different. At first she was intrigued by the dark, thick hair, then she came to believe that it "must not belong," because it had such a different color and texture. After a few weeks of pulling her pubic hair, she started to pull specific eyelashes that felt coarser or thicker as well. Over time, she realized that the smooth skin on her brow and eyelid felt nice without the prickly new hairs, and she pulled out any hair to achieve the smooth look and feeling of her skin. Now, when hair starts to grow in, she immediately pulls it because it feels sharp and pokey to her fingers, leaving her skin smooth and hair free.

Caitlin is a typical example of a child with hairpulling disorder (trichotillomania). Most children with hairpulling or skin-picking disorders pull or pick to reduce a negative sensory experience—for example, to remove all of the hairs that look or feel unusual or to achieve some pleasurable sensory experience, such as to look at the bulb on the end of the hair. Understanding that hairpulling and skin picking are self-soothing and self-regulating behaviors can help parents view these behaviors as more functional and less pathological, thus reducing their anxiety and increasing compassion for their child. Additionally, understanding the sensory element of a BFRB can help parents beef up alternative sensory soothing for their child, so that they will be less likely to seek out sensory soothing through the BFRB.

If your child is experiencing a BFRB, consider exploring multiple sensory soothers. To do this, think about all of the areas of the sensory nervous system—touch, taste, smell, sound, and sight. Fidgets that provide a smooth sensation, such as a smooth stone, a swatch of silky material, or a felt-covered ball may supply some sensory interest. Other sensations are worth exploring as well, such as putty that smells interesting, listening to music, chewing gum, a makeup brush to run along the face, cubes with multiple activities, textured kitchen items (sponges, vegetable brushes, or bottle brushes), or fidgets that provide some auditory interest. The lists go on and on. We want you to encourage your child to explore their sensory needs in a new way!

Attention Deficit Hyperactivity Disorder

Children with attention deficit hyperactivity disorder (ADHD) often have trouble maintaining attention, staying on task, completing multistep directions, completing and turning in homework assignments, organizing their rooms or backpacks, and remembering what they are supposed to be doing at a given moment. In addition, they display impulsive actions, often doing or saying things that they later regret. Children who have problems with sensory inhibition, discrimination, or habituation, sensory-processing problems discussed in chapter 2, may present with some of these same issues. These children often have difficulty with many other day-to-day actions:

- finding items in a desk, bag, or pocket

- locating items in a cupboard, drawer, or closet or on a grocery shelf

- recognizing, interpreting, or following traffic signs

- concentrating when there is background noise

- speaking at a reasonable volume

- judging how hard to push on objects, often breaking things

- telling time on an analog clock

- organizing things by categories

- lining up numbers correctly

- remembering what people are saying

- interrupting when another person is talking

- saying things without thinking first

- behaving impulsively

Children who are under-responsive to sensations may also have difficulty with sensory- seeking behaviors. These children often appear hyperactive, exhibiting behaviors such as:

- loving to touch and be touched

- fidgeting and fiddling with things all the time

- loving fast or dangerous rides and sports

- rocking or swaying body back and forth while seated or standing still

- tipping the chair back on two legs

- smelling or licking items to identify them

- chewing or sucking on things constantly—pencils, clothes, fingers

- constantly moving and not being able to sit still

- bouncing their leg up and down while sitting still

Although these children also have difficulty maintaining attention and concentration, consistent with ADHD, problems with sensory regulation are often also present. In other words, many children who have ADHD also have sensory regulation issues. For that reason, if your child has been diagnosed with ADHD, it is important to also look at their ability to regulate their sensory system to understand how best to approach helping them. As stated earlier, soothing the sensory system can also help reduce some of these problematic behaviors.

Soothing an ADHD nervous system can be fun and creative. Try exploring different sensory experiences to find which ones provide the right amount of stimulation, activity, and sensory soothing. Many times, engaging in sports that encourage movement and discipline, such as the martial arts, gymnastics, or track and field, may be helpful. Encourage your child to become an explorer of their body and senses so that you can work together as a team to solve the sensory regulation puzzle.

Autism Spectrum Disorders

Children with an autism spectrum disorder (ASD) often have developmental delays that are identified early on in life, usually by a pediatrician. There is also a range of more sensory-based problems associated with ASD:

- having trouble relating to others or not knowing how to interact interpersonally

- avoiding eye contact

- having trouble understanding other people's feelings or talking about their own feelings

- preferring not to be held or cuddled, or preferring cuddles only when they want it

- appearing to be unaware when people talk to them but responding to other sounds

- being interested in people, but not knowing how to talk, play, or relate to them

- having trouble with transitions or routine changes

- having unusual reactions to the way things smell, taste, look, feel, or sound

Children with ASD classically have problems with sensory regulation; it is a cornerstone of the disorder. Understanding the sensory system of a child with ASD is imperative to helping them function in a sensory-rich world. Calming the sensory system for children with ASD helps calm them in general and teaches them skills for managing a difficult sensory world.

Allison is an eleven-year-old girl in the fifth grade. She has been diagnosed with ASD, and she has been in a social skills group for the past three years. Her social skills have improved considerably, and she has a few friends whom she is very fond of. Her parents have always been patient with her, but they were confused about why she sometimes is able to manage her frustration, while other times she seems to completely break down and cry. Her mother used gentle inquiry to get a better understanding of the sensory aspects of these different environments to see whether she could better understand Allison's behavior. She asked, "Allison, tell me about yesterday, when you got upset during math class at school. What was different about that class?" Allison responded, "I don't know. I was just mad." Mom continued gently, "Well, I wonder what happened before that? Was there anything that was different that period?" Allison remembered, "Nothing really, except that Johnny threw up in the class before. It was disgusting, and I almost threw up too." Her mom continued, "Hmmm, was it the smell of the throw-up you did not like—or the sound or the look of it? What part did you not like?" Allison emphatically stated, "It is the smell, Mom! I can't stand the smell of puke. It makes me want to puke too!" Mom reflected, "Yes, that makes sense to me. Allison, you have always been sensitive to smells; remember how when you were little you used to love that lavender pillow? I wonder if you were upset that you had to smell that smell, and you got mad. Do you think the smell could have upset you?" Allison said, "Well maybe, because nothing else was really happening to upset me—I just felt mad." Mom offered, "Maybe we could put a bottle of lavender essential oil in your backpack so that you can smell that or put it under your nose if you ever have to be around bad smells. What do you think?" Allison beamed, "Yes, I would like that very much! I love the smell of lavender!"

Children on the spectrum always have some sensory sensitivities or needs. Fully understanding how to soothe your child is a great way to teach them how to regulate their systems and manage environments that are difficult for them. Knowing what is causing their discomfort and how to help alleviate it allows your child to feel powerful and gives them the tools they need to survive situations that are uncomfortable. The suggestions we are offering in this book are relevant both for children with ASD and for those who don't have it. Not all children with sensory regulation difficulties are on the autism spectrum, but all children on the spectrum have sensory regulation issues. If your child is on the autism spectrum, you will also likely need additional interventions to help with social and possibly academic functioning. As you are likely aware, children on the autism spectrum need more time to get used to new situations and experiences. This includes learning to self-soothe and tolerate difficult sensory experiences. So don't give up too soon! Remember that this is a process. You and your child will work with sensory-soothing experiences many, many times before you can expect an improvement in behavior.

Tourette Syndrome and Persistent Tic Disorders

Children with Tourette syndrome (TS) or persistent tic disorders (PTDs) have a range of tic behaviors, including vocal tics (throat clearing, grunting, sniffing, or saying certain words or syllables) and motor tics (facial grimaces, eye blinking, arm movements, or many complicated motor movements). Since tic disorders are neurological disorders, we know that the child's nervous system is functioning differently than children without tics; therefore, these children almost always have issues with sensory regulation.

If your child has a tic disorder, it can be helpful to look at their sensory system, understanding how they perceive different stimuli and how these perceptions impact their behaviors and emotions. With tics, it is always useful to understand what is soothing to your child and increase exposure to those items or activities, thus increasing their sense of being soothed, which can reduce the occurrence of tics. If you think about the child with tics as having a nervous system that is in a state of dysregulation, focusing on soothing and therefore regulating the nervous system is the best approach. This is why parents will report that their child's tics are better in some situations and worse in others. Many times it is the sensory aspects of these environments that increase or decrease the incidence of tics in that environment.

> Owen is ten years old and has been diagnosed with Tourette syndrome. He has both vocal and motor tics that are worse when he is in quiet environments, such as in the library, in class during tests, and in church. His parents have been frustrated because it is the times when everyone can hear his vocal tics that they are the worst. Owen's dad has been observing him patiently for several years, noticing what soothes his nervous system. He has noticed that when he is playing with putty his tics are decreased. Also, when he listens to his favorite music, he tends to experience the tics less frequently. He asked Owen if they could do an experiment: Owen would wear earbuds to listen to his favorite music and play with putty the next time they were in church. Surprisingly, Owen demonstrated only minimal tics during church that week. He later talked to Owen's teachers about having his earbuds and putty at school for when they go to the library and during tests. He explained, "It seems that Owen is not able to tolerate the silence and needs some sensory input when there is little noise." His teachers were willing to try this experiment but expressed concerns about his ability to focus on a test or to hear the librarian with earbuds in his ears. After the experiment, they learned that if he keeps the volume low, it provides enough input to help him manage his tics but does not distract him away from doing his work or listening to the teacher. It seems that his tics were actually more distracting to him than the music and the putty!

Each child with tics is different, so if your child has a tic disorder, remember to do a careful evaluation of their sensory system to see what they are seeking or avoiding so you can better understand what sensory changes might be effective. Using sensory soothing is not meant to be a replacement for the interventions for tic disorders, namely comprehensive behavioral intervention for tics (CBIT), but we have seen that it can help reduce tics in certain environments. Review the ABCs of your child's tics and see whether you can identify any environments that serve as an antecedent, so that the sensory aspects of this environment can be better understood.

Room for Soothing!

Something important to remember is the concept of the *Snoezelen* room discussed in chapter 1 of this book. The *Snoezelen* room is a multisensory concept from the Netherlands that refers to creating a room in your house that is completely soothing and relaxing to your senses. This room would have everything that makes your nervous system feel good—sounds, smells, colors, textures, and tastes. These rooms are uniquely tailored to soothe your nervous system. If you could create a *Snoezelen* room in your house for your child, what would it be like? Think of the colors, textures, smells, sounds, and tastes that your child might put there. We suggest making your child's bedroom a *Snoezelen* room, if at all possible. This is tricky for children sharing a room with a sibling, but we have found that selecting soothing items that appeal to both siblings is a good solution. In cases where siblings have very different sensory needs, we would recommend creating a "soothing tent" or "soothing corner" for each child to get their unique needs met. By making your child's room a sensory-soothing environment, you will be creating a safe space for them to relax, unwind, and recharge when needed. Remember, we think we know what is soothing, because we know our bodies, but what is soothing to you is not necessarily the same as what is soothing to your child. You and your child can "redecorate" their room by picking paint colors, blankets or comforters, pillows, diffusers, lights, noise-makers, and other items that make them feel good. Be creative, and don't worry about what it looks like to you—this is for them!

Conclusion

This chapter has examined several childhood disorders that are often accompanied by problems with sensory regulation. If your child has a BFRB, ADHD, ASD, or a PTD, they likely also have sensory-based issues. Understanding your child's sensory nervous system and then helping your child identify ways to soothe and regulate their nervous system is critical in helping them feel in control of their life experience. Regulating the nervous system helps children across the board, but with children who have these specific issues, it can be a game changer in terms of helping them reduce other problematic behaviors.

This concludes the first half of this book. In the first five chapters of this book we have outlined the nervous system; given you tools to understand your child and their sensory experience; explained how specific dysregulation can lead to problematic behaviors; reviewed specific sensory-based behaviors that are often misunderstood to be pediatric diagnoses; and reviewed specific childhood diagnoses that often also have sensory regulation problems. In the second half of this book, we will provide a step-by-step approach to help you help your child with sensory regulation. You will begin to use the information from the first half of this book to help you move toward solutions to these sensory glitches. The following is a helpful equation that combines interventions for sensory regulation with simple behavioral skills and will be described in detail in the next chapter:

Experience + Sensory Soothing + Coping Skills + Making It Fun
= Tolerance for the Sensory Triggers

This equation will be your recipe for success in helping your child move toward previously intolerable environments and, over time, be able to tolerate them. Skill building and tolerance for uncomfortable triggers help children feel powerful and face difficult situations while learning about themselves and developing self-compassion at the same time. This creative parenting approach, which uses tools for reducing anxiety, suggestions for soothing the dysregulated nervous system, and techniques that make this difficult process more fun, will be described in detail. With early intervention, children will develop important skills they can use throughout their lives, skills that lead to creative problem solving, better emotion regulation, reduced anxiety, increased functioning during stress, improved family relationships, more empathy toward others, and successful management of their nervous system.

PART 2

Helping Parents Help Their Child: Practical Applications

CHAPTER 6

Tools to Help Sensory Regulation
A Formula for Success

The chapters in part 1 of the book were primarily informational, explaining the workings of the nervous system and how problems with sensory regulation can disrupt a child's mood and behavior, can be mistaken for a childhood psychiatric disorder, and often co-occur with other disorders of childhood. This chapter describes how you as a parent can support, guide, and teach your child the tools they need to successfully navigate their world. Oftentimes well-meaning family members push a child to participate in the very activity that they have strong negative reactions to or have been avoiding. This thrust can trigger the sympathetic nervous system's response and can lead to anger and oppositional behavior (fight), avoidance (flight), or anxiety and shutting down (freeze), which affects the parent-child relationship. Helping a child understand why they are having an aversive reaction is an important step toward change. Children (and parents) feel validated and empowered once they understand how the child's unique nervous system works and, more importantly, how their reactions and feelings can be successfully managed. This chapter will provide a step-by-step guide for supporting your child, with examples along the way. Here is a sample of a more helpful kind of conversation—in this case, one Sally had with her mother after Sally had had a tough day at school with her friend Megan.

Mom: Tell me about what happened in school, Sally.

Sally: Megan got me in trouble with the teacher.

Mom:	So what happened to upset Megan?
Sally:	She just started to cry and yell at me.
Mom:	What did Megan say to you when she was crying?
Sally:	She said, "Stop it!"
Mom:	What was she referring to?
Sally:	Well, I was touching her hair. I like to touch her hair.
Mom:	Had she asked you to stop touching her hair before she started to cry?
Sally:	Yes, but I like to touch her hair. It's soft and feels good.
Mom:	I see. I think your hand tells you that it feels good to touch certain things. Is that right?
Sally:	That's right. I like the feel of soft things, like her hair.
Mom:	I see. Maybe we should find all sorts of soft things for you to touch so that your hand stays happy, and you feel good. But it's also important to listen when people tell you that they don't want to be touched. How about you and I go on a hunt for lots of soft things that you might like to touch?
Sally:	That would fun.
Mom:	Then we will put some of those things in your pockets and your desk at school so that you can touch those things when you need to touch something that feels soft, so you won't upset your friends.

Step 1: Educate

Simply providing information to your child about their likes and dislikes directly addresses the issue and leads to solutions. In other words, educate your child about their unique nervous system and how they might be an over- or under-responder to different sensory triggers. By now you probably have a good list of your child's sensory preferences and how they cope with or react to certain sensory triggers. In addition, it is important to normalize your child's experience without making them feel bad for either seeking out or avoiding specific sensations and situations. In cases where your child is engaging in potentially dangerous or inappropriate behaviors (e.g., licking non-food items or touching themselves or others inappropriately), help them set boundaries that keep them safe and socially appropriate. Let your child know that while these behaviors may feel good to them, not all behaviors are a good idea, even if they feel good. This way, you can guide your child to know limits of behavior and how to manage their nervous system in better ways. Remind your child about their sensory preferences and use the information you have gathered thus far to help them understand why they feel the way they do and why they respond the way they do. Once you have a good grasp of your child's sensory nervous system, you will be able to provide your child with safe and more socially appropriate ways to get their needs met, thus helping them have a more positive sensory experience overall.

To sum up the first step in helping your child (Educate), you will want to:

1. teach your child about their unique nervous system and explain why they respond the way they do in specific situations and to certain sensory triggers;

2. review any limits you want to encourage on their behaviors using specific examples (for example, things they've done in the past that were inappropriate or possibly dangerous); and

3. explain to your child about how it may seem to them that these behaviors are the answer (for example, licking the bottom of their shoe to see what it tastes like), but that they could be dangerous—and encourage your child that you will help them find other things to do and ways to manage these difficult situations.

The next step—and the focus of the rest of this book—is to figure out what to do to support your child in sensory environments that have caused problems in the past. The following formula is your road map to success in helping your child get comfortable with difficult sensory environments and, thus, improve functioning for the entire family:

Experience + Sensory Soothing + Coping Skills + Making It Fun
= Tolerance for the Sensory Triggers

The remainder of this chapter will focus in detail on how to use the individual pieces of the above formula, explaining how they can bolster your child's ability to tolerate difficult sensory experiences and reengage with the world.

Step 2: Experience

Experience refers to facing the thing that is hard for them—in other words, helping your child experience the sensory triggers that are difficult for them (noises, smells, tastes, touch sensations, or movements). Experience is the first step in moving toward more healthy interactions with the environment, but it cannot be done before introducing other important skills. Simply introducing the sensory experience that is diffi- cult, without also teaching ways to cope with it, is a losing strategy, and probably one that you have tried in the past. Experience might involve creating a system to enable tasting foods that are objectionable, going into a smelly bathroom, or allowing the fire alarm to ring and not escape, but not before arming them with the skills that allow your child to succeed.

Where do you start? Most children with sensory regulation issues have multiple areas that are problematic. We recommend starting with a sensory trigger that is a problem, but not the worst one. In other words, avoid starting with the sensory trigger that is the hardest for your child to tolerate, mainly because we want you and your child to have a successful first go at this.

Take a Moment: Look back in your journal and ABCs of Behavior Chart from chapter 3. Review the antecedents (what happened before the behavior started) to identify all of your child's sensory triggers. Note all of the places, smells, sounds, and other sensations that seem to cause your child to act out. Make a list of all of these sensory triggers or environments. Now, use the following Rating Your Child's Sensory Triggers Chart to help you categorize them.

Rating Your Child's Sensory Triggers Chart

	Mild (1–3)	Moderate (4–7)	Severe (8–10)
Seldom			
Sometimes			
All the Time			

There are three columns, labeled "Mild (1–3)," "Moderate (4–7)," and "Severe (8–10)" which refers to how hard this trigger is for your child on a scale of 1 to 10, with 10 being the most difficult. Now, on the left-hand side you will see the chart's three rows labeled "Seldom," "Sometimes," and "All the Time." This refers to how frequently your child has to be in this situation or how frequently this trigger is a problem. Put each trigger in one of the boxes. For example, if your child reacts severely to fire alarms, but a fire alarm rings only once every few months, you would put fire alarms in the "Seldom–Severe" box like this:

	Mild (1–3)	Moderate (4–7)	Severe (8–10)
Seldom			Fire Alarms
Sometimes			
All the Time			

However, if your child has a severe reaction to fire alarms, and even though the alarms are rare, your child fears hearing them so much that they are refusing to go to school, you would put fire alarms in the "All the Time–Severe" box, as in the example below:

	Mild (1–3)	Moderate (4–7)	Severe (8–10)
Seldom			
Sometimes			
All the Time			Fire Alarms

Go through your list and place each trigger in the appropriate box. The purpose of this chart is to help you both see a comprehensive list of all the triggers you will want to work on and to guide you to the best place to begin. You would not want to start with the most severe and most frequent trigger, because it would be too overwhelming—just as you would not start training for a marathon by heading out one morning and running twenty miles. We want you to pick something that is fairly frequent and moderately difficult. When in doubt, select ones that happen more frequently, but are not the most severe.

Once you have decided which sensory trigger to target first, you can begin to make your Experience Ladder. An Experience Ladder is a step-wise approach for confronting the sensory experience, starting with easy (low on the ladder) and moving up the ladder to harder and harder experiences. Each sensory trigger will have a separate Experience Ladder in the beginning. For the purpose of illustration, let's look at Tammy, a six-year-old with tactile sensitivities who is particular about what clothing she will wear. These issues are not the most severe issues that she struggles with, but they affect her almost daily when dressing for school and other activities. Tammy's ABCs of Behavior Chart details the problems.

Tammy's ABCs of Behavior Chart

Antecedents	Behaviors	Consequences
She feels like her underwear, shorts, and shirts are tight, itchy, and very uncomfortable.	She refuses to wear anything except for one shirt and two pairs of shorts. She refuses to wear underwear.	Kids at school tease her for always wearing the same clothing. Mom washes her preferred clothing daily.

So, her mother recorded this trigger in the Rating Your Child's Sensory Triggers Chart as All the Time–Moderate as illustrated below:

	Mild (1–3)	Moderate (4–7)	Severe (8–10)
Seldom			
Sometimes			
All the Time		Wear Underwear	

The next step in developing the Experience Ladder is to break down the sensory trigger experience into many steps, so that your child can begin with an easy-to-manage challenge and move to progressively harder ones. Using the above example, Tammy and her parents talk about what would be really, really hard to wear, what would be only slightly hard to wear, and everything in between. Tammy decided that wearing underwear, jeans, and a sweater to school for the whole day would be a 10, the absolute hardest thing to do. She then decided that wearing really soft underwear under her shorts for one hour would probably be the easiest thing to do. They began to make an Experience Ladder that ended up looking like this:

Tammy's Experience Ladder

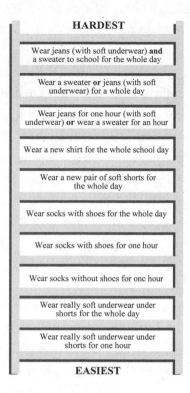

HARDEST

Wear jeans (with soft underwear) **and** a sweater to school for the whole day

Wear a sweater **or** jeans (with soft underwear) for a whole day

Wear jeans for one hour (with soft underwear) **or** wear a sweater for an hour

Wear a new shirt for the whole school day

Wear a new pair of soft shorts for the whole day

Wear socks with shoes for the whole day

Wear socks with shoes for one hour

Wear socks without shoes for one hour

Wear really soft underwear under shorts for the whole day

Wear really soft underwear under shorts for one hour

EASIEST

As you can see, by starting at the bottom and moving up the Experience Ladder, the tasks get harder and harder to do, with number 10 being the absolute hardest. Tammy should practice each step or activity until she masters it before moving up the ladder to the next step or activity. Moving up too quickly could make Tammy feel frustrated and overwhelmed, but successfully wearing her soft underwear under her shorts for an hour without an adverse reaction will give her a sense of confidence and accomplishment. She will be more likely to look to the next challenge with the feeling *I can do this!* Initially while going through her ladder, Tammy should be able to choose highly desirable clothing for her experiences, like a T-shirt that has a cat on it that is not only very soft, but also really cute. She would be allowed to select her own underwear and socks that are very soft. This not only gives Tammy a sense of control during this process, but it also makes the experience more of a treat, rather than simply a challenge.

Now that your first Experience Ladder is complete, *stop!* Before actually encouraging your child to take on the first challenge of the Experience Ladder, it is necessary for you to teach your child some skills to help along the way. This ladder is an excellent beginning, but most children find that simply experiencing the sensation, even in small increments, is not enough to help them move toward successful tolerance of sensory triggers. By adding the following important tools, you can make the experience fun, manageable, and, most importantly, successful.

Step 3: Sensory Soothing

When children experience problems with sensory regulation, they are prisoners of their own internal reactions. They are often confused and don't know how to make sense of a world wrought with so many uncomfortable sensory experiences. Providing sensory experiences that either compete with or distract a child from discomfort can help reduce the negative experience and make the exposure more tolerable. Sensory soothing refers to either providing a pleasant sensory experience to compete with the unpleasant one (such as holding a peppermint-scented handkerchief to your face when you have to go into a smelly bathroom) or simply creating a positive sensory experience that is similar to the target (like sucking on a mint instead of licking an object), but more appropriate.

Let's go back to the example of Tammy to illustrate what we mean. Before beginning to work on her Experience Ladder, Tammy and her parents would want to start exploring which types of sensory experiences she might find soothing. Some examples that Tammy identified were listening to her favorite music, the smell of lavender and peppermint, feeling something smooth (like a piece of satin or a smooth stone), and chewing gum. Tammy was then instructed to practice using sensory soothing while working on her Experience Ladder, such as using earbuds to listen to her favorite music during the school day (with the volume low enough that she could still hear her teacher and the other students), having lavender and peppermint essential oils with her to smell when she is feeling uncomfortable, rubbing a smooth stone in her hand during class, and chewing her favorite gum (all with permission from the school). All of these sensory experiences help calm Tammy down and help her regulate her nervous system, while she is tolerating the different challenges on her Experience Ladder. Adding sensory soothing to offset the sensory irritation is a key component to success. As with all items and skills you may introduce to your child, be aware of your child's age and development. Small children are at risk for choking, so gum, hard candy, unsupervised essential oils, and small items may not be appropriate at this age. There are lots of options. Don't be afraid to be creative!

What soothes your child? Here is a list of sensations or sensory items that are good ideas to use to regulate your child's nervous system.

- *Touch:* soft blanket, squishy ball, cool slime, furry stuffed animal, sandpaper, spiky balls, bottle brush, smooth stone or fabric, putty, smooth magnets

- *Smell:* vanilla, cinnamon sticks, essential oils, perfume, diffusers

- *Sound:* nature sounds, classical music, rock music, country music, white noise, noise-canceling headphones, storm sounds

- *Visual:* light colors, dark colors, bright colors, whites, solids, stripes, patterns (plaid or paisley), dim lights, bright lights, sunglasses (to reduce light)

- *Taste:* gum, hard candy with strong flavors, mints, butterscotch, cream flavors

These or other sensory items your child prefers will be soothing tools to assist your child in moving up their Experience Ladder. Make a list, with the assistance of your child, of the sensory soothers that they will want to use and make sure that you have them all on hand. You may need to purchase some items such as essential oils or smooth stones or other things. Craft stores and kitchen supply stores are excellent places to find interesting sensory objects. Take your child with you to shop so that they can try things out and advise you about what feels, smells, tastes, sounds, and looks good. It is helpful to introduce the use of sensory-soothing items before approaching the Experience Ladder. Practice using the sensory items daily and always have them on hand, if at all possible. Getting in the habit of using these items before starting work on the Experience Ladder will help your child prepare for the challenges of the ladder. You want to make sure that your child knows from experience how soothing the items are, so they are confident of having those tools at hand when they begin the first challenge.

Step 4: Teach Coping Skills

Coping skills include techniques such as relaxation, deep breathing, and coping statements that can be used before, during, and after difficult experiences. Once coping skills have been practiced and mastery has been achieved, you can begin to encourage your child to work on the first rung of the Experience Ladder.

Relaxation

Relaxation training is an important tool to use when learning self-regulation. Children who are over-responsive become extremely uncomfortable quickly when their sympathetic nervous system is activated. The discomfort is confusing and frightening, and it provokes anxiety, particularly if the fight-flight-or-freeze response is triggered. Relaxation skills can help reduce muscle tension, slow down breathing, and calm the nervous system.

Relaxation training helps children slow down their emotional and physical reactions and calm their bodies. It is particularly useful with sensory over-responsive children (those who avoid sensory experiences), as it helps them achieve the needed sense of calm in situations that were previously intolerable. Sensory-seeking children (those who touch, smell, lick, fidget, and otherwise seek out stimulation) also benefit from relaxation because this gives them an internal sensory focus rather than solely relying on external sources of sensory input. The core concept of relaxation practice for children is to focus on relaxing different body parts while breathing deeply and slowly. The following is a simple relaxation exercise that you can read to your child to practice:

Close your eyes, make sure your body is comfortable by uncrossing your legs and arms, and find a comfortable position where you are seated. Now, focus on your breathing. Just notice how your breath feels as it goes in and out through your nose [pause ten seconds]. *Notice how your stomach goes in and out as your breath goes in and out* [pause ten seconds]. *Now, I want you to start with your head and notice the muscles in your scalp, face, mouth, and cheeks. Notice how they feel. Now, I want you to tense these muscles: scrunch up your face and mouth and hold it* [hold for five seconds]. *Now let it go. Notice how your muscles feel to let go of tension, to relax. Again, tense up the muscles of your scalp, mouth, and face and hold it* [hold for five seconds]. *Now let it go. Again, notice how your muscles feel to let go of tension, to relax. Now move to the muscles of your neck and shoulders: tense up these muscles by raising your shoulders toward your ears and tilting your head toward your upper back and hold it* [hold for five seconds]. *Now relax. Notice how your muscles feel to let go of tension, to relax. Again, tense the muscles of your neck and shoulders and hold* [hold for five seconds], *and relax. Now move to the muscles of your arms and hands: straighten your arms and clench your fists and hold it tight* [hold for five seconds]. *Now relax. Again, tense up your arms and hands* [hold for five seconds], *and relax. Now move to the muscles of your stomach and chest: clench up these muscles and hold it* [hold for five seconds], *and relax. Again, tense up the muscles of your stomach and back and hold* [hold for five seconds], *and relax. Now move to the muscles of your legs: tense up the muscles of your thighs and hold* [hold for five seconds], *and relax. Let go of all of the tension in your thighs. Again, tense up the muscles of your thighs and hold* [hold for five seconds], *and relax. Now, move to the muscles of your calves and shins: tense these muscles and hold* [hold for five seconds]. *Now relax. Again, tense these muscles* [hold for five seconds], *and relax. Finally, tense the muscles of your feet and toes and hold* [hold for five seconds]. *Now relax. Again, tense these muscles and hold* [hold for five seconds], *and relax. Now, scan your entire body and notice how it feels, how relaxed your muscles feel. If there are any muscles that still feel tense, go ahead and tense them even more and hold* [hold for five seconds], *and then relax. Notice the difference in how it feels to have tense muscles and to have muscles that are relaxed.*

Many children might find listening to a relaxation app or download easier than working with a parent. Sometimes it can work well to have child and parent listen together to a relaxation exercise. If possible, practice doing this relaxation exercise every day. Daily practice helps increase awareness of one's body and how it is feeling. Start by doing this exercise during a naturally relaxing time, such as after a bath or in bed before sleep. This will enhance relaxation and help "teach" the body how to relax. With practice, your child will become better at noticing tension and helping their body relax more naturally. With very young children, you might try a different relaxation strategy. You might make these exercises like a game by asking them to be as straight and rigid as possible, like an uncooked spaghetti noodle, and to hold this for five seconds. Then, ask your child to "cook" in their seat, allowing their body to become pliable like a cooked noodle. What happens to their arms and legs? How floppy can they become? Tightening the muscles while being rigid and relaxing them while pretending to be an overcooked noodle illustrates the concepts of muscle relaxation for a younger child. With younger children, the noodle image can also become a cue that a parent can give to their child. If you notice that your child is tense, you can give the prompt "Let's cook noodles!" to remind them to relax their body.

Breathing Practice

When teaching breathing skills to young children (younger than age five), you might start with blowing bubbles. By instructing your youngster how to take a big breath in, purse the lips, and blow slowly and steadily through the bubble ring, your child can learn how to engage their diaphragm and support blowing out a long, slow breath. Pretend together that you are blowing bubbles to practice the deep breathing skill. Encourage them to picture lots of bubbles floating around as they blow. Encourage your young child to practice deep breathing each morning and evening. When you see them struggling during the day, this is a great time to give a reminder to "blow some bubbles" to help calm a tense body. With practice, your child will eventually start to remember to blow bubbles all by themselves, whenever they are feeling tense.

For children older than age five, we recommend teaching them to practice breathing with counting. We recommend counting to five while breathing in through the nose, holding the breath for three counts, then counting to five while exhaling through the mouth, and finally holding for three counts. In for five, hold for three, out for five, hold for three. Continue with the counting and breathing for ten full breath cycles. Again, this can be done in both the morning and the evening. Sometimes it helps when you practice doing the breathing with your child to model how it is done and to reinforce practice. Another approach is to find an app that teaches deep breathing to children. There are many good options out there. You and your child might spend some time exploring. No matter which strategy is used, the method for the deep breathing should be practiced until your child feels comfortable using the skill.

Coping Statements

Many children experience maladaptive or scary thoughts when they know they have to face unpleasant sensory environments, such as *This is going to be terrible!* or *I can't do this!* It is helpful to discover the content of these thoughts so that they can be challenged. If the thoughts that occur with regard to sensory experiences are inaccurate (*I am going to die!* or *This is the worst thing that could ever happen!*), you and your child could work together to create more accurate statements that correct these thoughts, such as *I am not dying; I just feel uncomfortable right now* or *This is not my favorite feeling, but I can handle this* or *Socks are not my favorite, but I will wear them today.* It may be helpful to refer to this self-talk as "best-friend" talk. Children should be instructed to say to themselves only the kind of statements that they would say to their best friend in that situation. They would probably not say "This is the worst thing that could ever happen to you!" to their best friend, but rather something like "This is not so bad. You can do it!" Some examples of common coping or best-friend statements are as follows:

- This is uncomfortable, but it will pass.

- You can do this.

- You are strong. You can handle this.

- Just relax and focus on something else. You got this!

- You are doing great! Keep it up.

- You are working so hard, keep going!

Accurate statements that describe a child's nervous system can also be helpful, such as *I have a sensitive sense of smell; Most loud sounds are not dangerous, just loud;* or *Certain things bother me more than they bother other people.* Finally, they can repeat statements affirming that they have the ability to use their new tools and resources, such as *I can do my deep breathing, I can relax my muscles,* and *Smelling the perfume on my wrist will make this bathroom smell better so I can tolerate it for the next three minutes.* All of these skills help children reduce their anxiety-provoking thoughts, which will help them cope better in difficult situations. Talk to your child about their self-talk and help them modify it. Prompt your child to use coping statements when confronting challenging sensory sensations.

Step 5: Make It Fun!

One of the most important ingredients in the formula for tolerance of sensory triggers is to make it fun. Making this kind of experience fun is critical to engaging your child and ultimately getting them to participate. Using fun games helps lessen the negative response to the sensory experience and increases motivation to approach behaviors that were previously avoided. Games are fun, exciting, and rewarding, which improves compliance and makes this process more enjoyable.

For example, Tammy might play "beat the clock" while wearing her soft underwear. She might set a goal of wearing the underwear for one hour (the first challenge on her Experience Ladder). Her parent would set a timer for one hour, and then, when the timer goes off, Tammy can either take them off or continue on. Either way, she was successful at beating the clock. The next time, she would set the clock for a longer period and try to beat it. Each time she is able to beat the clock, she would earn larger prizes or points for her success.

Making it fun is about changing how you approach the uncomfortable situation by making it a game or somehow making it silly. It can help take the pressure off both you and your child, and it can make these experiences more tolerable for your child, thus improving participation. Some good examples of ways to make challenges fun are as follows:

- Play music while brushing teeth. Your child has to brush for the whole song.

- Have a fashion show in the living room to practice wearing clothing with different textures.

- Dance to the tune of the unpleasant noise. See who can dance the funniest.

- Play "name that smell." Smell different things and see who can guess what the smell might be.

- Play "clean your plate" with other family members, with prizes for the first-, second-, and third-place finishers.

- Dance to the sound of the alarm going off, as if it were a favorite song.

- Play a "statue game." Everyone is completely still like a statue and the first one to move loses.

Sometimes, especially with older children, playing a game is not appealing or is simply not enough to keep them engaged. In such cases, you may have to develop a reward system to provide immediate and long-term positive reinforcement for your child's active participation. The next section will explain how to develop and implement a successful reward system to encourage your child to engage in this process.

Developing a Reward System

Positive reinforcement helps children engage in moving up their Experience Ladder more consistently and more readily. Immediate, desirable rewards are critical for many children to engage in this difficult process. Rewards can be either verbal, physical, or tangible. Specific verbal feedback from parents or caregivers is the easiest way to reinforce positive behaviors and should always be done first. Notice your child's efforts and comment on them immediately, whenever you see them occur: "Great job eating those peas and carrots," "Fantastic use of deep breathing," and "I am really proud of how you used the restroom at the restaurant." Notice how all of the feedback is focused on the new behaviors rather than the old behaviors. We don't want to comment on non-behaviors, such as "You didn't cry this time" or "Look, you did not run away." We want to reinforce the replacement behaviors rather than remind them of the things they used to do. What *did* your child do? "Great job rubbing that smooth stone. You were able to keep your hands to yourself! Way to go!" See the difference? This is an important point when helping your child change their behavior.

Physical rewards are also a great way to show your child that you observe their effort and are proud of them. Give a literal pat on the back, a hug, a huge smile, a wink, or some hearty applause (depending on the age and preferences of your child) to show your approval and your excitement at their efforts and their successes. Children need to know that their efforts have been seen and that you are happy and proud of them. If they are working hard and get no feedback from you, they will be confused and often will stop making these efforts. It is important that you recognize their effort in some positive way if you want them to continue working to change their behavior and take on the challenges of the Experience Ladder.

Tangible reward systems help children develop motivation to participate in this process, endure difficult steps along the way, and navigate the process of behavior change. Reward systems seem easy to create, but, in reality, they take some time, energy, and effort to develop well. Most often when reward systems fail, it is because they were poorly designed, too complicated, difficult to maintain, or inconsistently executed. Many parents mention rewards but fail to adequately develop a system or do not follow through. Because reward systems can be hard to create, many well-intentioned parents fall victim to creating systems in which behavioral expectations are vague, expectations are too high, rewards are too hard to earn or take too long to earn, rewards are not gratifying for the child, or parents simply forget to give the rewards.

In order to create an effective reward system, you will need to plan ahead and gather small rewards to keep on hand. Talk to your child about small items or special activities that could be fun to earn. Special activities could be anything your child especially enjoys or craves:

- special time with one parent

- playing a game with a parent (e.g., checkers or card games)

- going out for a meal with a parent or the whole family

- having a favorite item for dinner (such as mashed potatoes or chicken prepared in a specific way)

- inviting a friend over for dinner or a sleepover

- movie night with family or friends

- going out to the movies

- ice skating, bowling, or any other fun activity

Small rewards include anything your child is especially excited about:

- art supplies

- games

- books

- pieces of clothing

- inexpensive jewelry

- toy cars, planes, or trains

After talking with your child and hearing their ideas for rewards, make a list of those items that would be fun to earn. Prepare by purchasing these items and having them ready to give to your child when they begin working on their Experience Ladder. Sometimes families start this process before they have a supply of rewards in the home. This lack of preparation leads to frustration on the part of the child and is a good example of how reward systems can quickly fall apart. Again, be prepared with your plan in place and your rewards at hand to make for a successful program!

The second—and more important—aspect of a reward system is to make the behavioral expectations crystal clear. An expectation of "wear a greater variety of clothing" might seem specific enough but is entirely too vague for most children. More specific and, we would argue, better expectations might be:

- Wear your pink underwear for ten minutes.

- Wear a dress to Grandma and Grandpa's house for dinner.

- Wear socks with your shoes for one hour.

- Wear a different pair of shorts each day for one week.

Specific goals are measurable, making it is easier to know whether they have been achieved. Vague and unspecific goals are hard to quantify and hard to measure, and therefore lead to arguments and confusion. Once specific behaviors are targeted, write them down in a form that is easy to follow and allows you to easily record progress. A chart is usually the best way to achieve this. Think about where the chart will be kept (somewhere that is easily visible is usually most effective), as well as when the chart should be filled out (at a specified time each day). You and your child will decide which behaviors to target for change each week, based on the Experience Ladder. A sample reward chart might look like this:

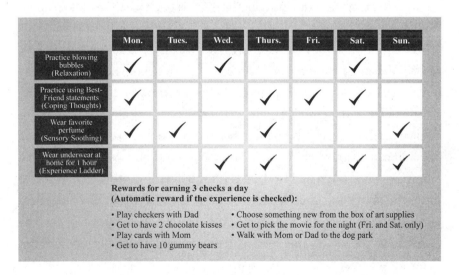

	Mon.	Tues.	Wed.	Thurs.	Fri.	Sat.	Sun.
Practice blowing bubbles (Relaxation)	✓		✓			✓	
Practice using Best-Friend statements (Coping Thoughts)	✓			✓	✓	✓	
Wear favorite perfume (Sensory Soothing)	✓	✓		✓			✓
Wear underwear at home for 1 hour (Experience Ladder)			✓	✓		✓	✓

**Rewards for earning 3 checks a day
(Automatic reward if the experience is checked):**

- Play checkers with Dad
- Get to have 2 chocolate kisses
- Play cards with Mom
- Get to have 10 gummy bears

- Choose something new from the box of art supplies
- Get to pick the movie for the night (Fri. and Sat. only)
- Walk with Mom or Dad to the dog park

Another strategy that works for many parents is to give points for different achievements. We use this strategy a lot for children who are rigid and who need to work toward being more flexible. Children are able to earn "flexibility points" for doing things that demonstrate adaptable thinking and easy going behavior:

- staying calm when plans change

- being willing to play a game that is different than what they want to play

- being willing to share when they have struggled in the past

- being open to new ideas, places, or experiences

- when given a choice, responding with "either is fine with me!"

- not becoming angry or frustrated when told no when they want something

- approaching challenges on their Experience Ladder

Making flexibility part of your everyday language and a goal to earn points for is tremendously helpful in teaching rigid children how to be flexible. Remember in the introduction of this book when we talked about "raw spaghetti" versus "cooked spaghetti"? Children who are "raw spaghetti" break when they are bent. Breaking usually looks like anger, crying, rage, or defiance, and it typically occurs when things are not going the way a child expects or wants them to go. What we know is that children who have trouble with sensory regulation also have rigid minds and tend to behave like "raw spaghetti." Children who are "cooked spaghetti" are flexible and can adapt when needed. These children can tolerate when plans change or when Mom and Dad are serving something other than pizza for dinner. Helping your child learn to be flexible is often key to helping them be more adaptive in life. Giving points for flexible behavior or for any actions that reflect working toward their goals can be an easy approach to a reward system.

Keys to success with a point system are:

- Parents must be vigilant and look for changes in their child's behavior so that they can administer the points. The burden is on the parent to watch for change.

- Points must be awarded immediately, whether that takes place on a phone or on a chart.

- Points must translate into something tangible for the child, such as *one point = some specified amount of money or something else* or *one hundred points equals a gift card to the child's favorite store.*

- Each week, points should be tallied and rewards delivered so that the child experiences the benefits of their hard work. If you forget to give the reward, you undermine the reward system altogether.

Step 6: Putting It All Together

Now that you have all of the ingredients for the success formula, let's put it together to make a successful plan of action to help your child build their tolerance for sensory triggers. Begin by helping your child grow their internal resources. Encourage the use of the sensory-soothing strategies that you have purchased by making them readily available—put them in your child's room, in their backpack, in the car, in the family room, and in your own purse or pockets. Practice using the sensory-soothing tools every day. Next, begin to teach relaxation and deep breathing exercises. Practice relaxation exercises at night before bed. At this point, you can add best-friend coping statements. You and your child can read them together (or you can read them to a young child who is not yet reading) at night after relaxation exercises. This is an excellent time to start using the reward system. Create a chart that lists the different skills that you want them to use, with spaces for them to put a check mark or point when they are completed. Your child will earn a check or a point, for example, each time they use one of the skills and each time they do the targeted behavior.

Now you are ready to start the Experience Ladder and begin to work from easier to harder experiences. Review the experiences you have written down in your journal and the Rating Your Child's Sensory Triggers Chart at the start of this chapter. Remember, choose a sensory trigger that is not severe but that is fairly frequent. Talk with your child to decide where to begin. You may have an idea of where your child will want to start, but they may tell you differently. Once you have decided together, you can then begin to build your first Experience Ladder. Start by identifying the easiest and the hardest tasks to do, then place them at the 1 and the 10 positions. Next, start to fill in the levels in between. Things that can make it easier or harder are to limit the time spent experiencing the trigger or wearing earplugs if approaching sound is the target behavior. Be sure to make the earlier experiences (1 to 4) doable, so that your child will be more open to trying them and will be more likely to succeed. Success at the first experience is crucial—it will fill your child with confidence and a sense of accomplishment. And it will encourage them to continue working on the other challenges.

Once the Experience Ladder is written out and agreed upon, combine the practice with the coping skills. For Tammy, it might look like this:

Tammy's Experience Ladder, first step:

1. Wear soft underwear under shorts for one hour while listening to your favorite music and fidgeting with a smooth stone (sensory soothing). Practice relaxation exercises and best-friend statements (coping skills).

Tammy could earn three points for this step (make it fun): one point for wearing underwear, one point for using sensory-soothing strategies, and one point for practicing coping skills. Remember, sensory soothing should be used while your child is doing the target activities, as well as during activities not related to the Experience Ladder. Sensory-soothing activities are good to use at any time, both while working on the Experience Ladder and when not working on it.

You may need to encourage participation and help ease the difficulty of the ladder by adding a game to the experience. For Tammy, she and her parents decided that in addition to rubbing a smooth stone, breathing deeply, and telling herself, *You got this!* she also was open to having a dance party (listening to music) with her friend for this one hour. Her mother planned to have her best friend over (one who knew about her goals of working on wearing more clothing alternatives) so that they could have a dance party to make this hour more fun. Her mom made a playlist of all of her favorite dance songs to further distract her from her discomfort. As a result, Tammy's first challenge on the Experience Ladder was fun and less stressful than if she had attempted it on a school day or if she had been doing it alone at home, when she would not have had the fun distraction of a dance party with her friend.

Each Experience Ladder and each set of sensory soothers, coping skills, games, and rewards will look different for each child and family. In addition, new target behaviors will require a different Experience Ladder with different tools to help.

So far in this chapter we have been focusing on kids who are reactive to sensory stimuli, but what about sensory seekers?

Sensory Seekers

Many of the examples illustrated in this chapter have been of children who are over-responsive, those who typically avoid or react negatively to unpleasant sensory experiences. As a result, the goals have focused on getting your child to be able to move toward or tolerate unpleasant sensory experiences. What about the sensory seekers? When children are under-responsive and need lots of sensory stimulation to feel good, the approach is the same, but sometimes the goals are a little different. The Experience Ladder might be geared toward sitting with hands occupied with sensory items in the classroom, without touching other students, or chewing gum while resisting licking inappropriate objects. In the case of sensory seeking, use the same formula, but the goal is to reduce problematic behaviors by giving lots of strong sensory input.

Remember Keesha from the introduction of this book? Keesha was constantly touching, smelling, licking, and bothering her peers to give her the sensory stimulation she needed to feel comfortable. Her Experience Ladder might be geared toward keeping her hands to herself during class (on the high end) and walking through the grocery store without touching anything (on the low end). In order to achieve this lower step, she might smell a pouch flavored with strong peppermint, rub a rough object like sandpaper or a special lava stone, and listen to loud dance music through her headphones while walking through the grocery store. Her mother might have her pretend that she is a tightrope walker and that she has to walk down the center of the aisle to "stay on the tightrope." This activity alone would make it harder to wander close to the groceries in the aisles and touch the many interesting items on the shelves.

We will talk more about this in the next chapter, but we wanted to remind you that even though some of the content may seem a little different, the process is much the same for children with an under-responsive nervous system as it is for those with an over-responsive system. In addition, keep in mind that children are complex and sometimes are both over-responsive to some sensory experiences and under-responsive to others. If this is the case for your child, create Experience Ladders that are geared to both types of behavior while adding in coping strategies and making it fun.

Conclusion

Helping your child successfully tolerate environments that are challenging from a sensory perspective is a gift that will help them for the remainder of their life. This chapter has outlined how to take information gathered in previous chapters and apply it to the formula for successful tolerance for sensory triggers. You learned how to prioritize which behaviors to address first and, once you have decided what to target, how to build an Experience Ladder to help your child approach harder and harder tasks. You then learned how to teach your child to soothe their senses, relax and breathe, and use coping statements, and you learned how to make this whole process fun and rewarding to keep your child actively engaged while doing this hard work. The next chapter will explain interventions that are used for specific sensory sensitivities and how to incorporate them into the treatment formula discussed in this chapter.

CHAPTER 7

Specific Tools to Help Under- and Over-Responsive Children

Now that you have a better understanding of the formula for success, we want to take a closer look at specific tools that can be useful for you, depending on the struggles your child is facing with sensory regulation. This chapter explores the internal experience of children who are either over- or under-responsive to various forms of sensory input. We provide multiple tools for each sense to help you build your child's toolbox. Because each child is different, some of the sections in this chapter will be relevant to your child, and some may seem unrelated to the struggles your child experiences. If a section feels like it is not relevant to the struggles your child has, feel free to skip that section and focus on the parts that pertain to your child's sensory issues. To increase tolerance for sensory triggers, you must combine experience with sensory soothing, coping skills, and making it fun. Remember the formula for success we discussed in the last chapter.

Experience + Sensory Soothing + Coping Skills + Making It Fun
= Tolerance for the Sensory Triggers

The Far Senses

Olfactory

Children who have a lack of sensitivity to smell can under-experience odors, which may lead to poor awareness of personal hygiene, seeking out strong odors, smelling everything they encounter, and not noticing foul odors when other children are reacting to them. On the other hand, some children over-respond to smells, which may cause them to avoid environments with strong smells, such as public restrooms, barns, places with chemical smells, or even the school cafeteria. On the other end of the spectrum, the sensory-seeking side, these smelling, licking, and tasting behaviors can be seen as unusual or strange by other people, and children with these issues typically experience negative social feedback.

Tools that can be used to address under-responsiveness to smell may include setting a schedule for regular showers, routine use of deodorant, and rules about laundering clothes after they have been worn once. While most children can smell their clothes and determine when they need to be laundered, children with an under-responsive nose have trouble determining when something smells or smells strong enough to warrant washing. Creating a schedule and rules that do not rely on the sense of smell are good techniques to use with these under-responsive children. For example, a child with an under-responsive nose might have these guidelines placed on them:

- put all clothes in the laundry after being worn once (except for dress clothing)

- shower or take a bath every night

- wash hair at least every other day

- use deodorant every day (if the child is at an appropriate age)

- follow the rules and don't trust your nose

Give rewards for sticking to the schedule to increase motivation. Behavior charts that track compliance with check marks or stickers can be useful, as the child will be able to see how far they have come and what they need to do to earn a prize.

Sometimes children who are under-responsive to smell will seek out strong smells for sensory soothing or smell inappropriate objects that they come into contact with. If this is the case for your child, try offering strong, pleasant-smelling alternatives, such as scented lotions, essential oils, or perfume on the wrists that can be easily smelled when your child needs some olfactory input. Smelling a wrist allows your child to get this need met without subjecting them to social criticism. Allowing them to chew strong-flavored gum or suck on very sour candy can also satisfy this need. These strong smells and tastes serve as a sensory distraction as well as providing interesting sensory input, so your child will be less compelled to seek out smells in unconventional ways. Again, verbal praise and tangible rewards encourage behavior change. Be careful to never judge your child when they lapse and smell inappropriate things, like the bottom of their shoe—remember that the behavior is simply a way your child soothes their nervous system. When that happens, gently remind them that they are trying to learn new ways and ask them if they remember the perfume on their wrist or the sour candy they have ready in their pocket. Be supportive and helpful, never judgmental or shaming.

Over-responsive children, on the other hand, have trouble entering spaces with strong smells, but they benefit from using these same sensory-soothing tools (wearing essential oils, pleasant smelling lotions, perfume, or a pleasant-smelling aftershave on their wrists). In addition to having pleasant smells available at all times, have strong good smells available when they are forced to enter a place with a bad smell. For example, if you are cutting up or cooking onions and garlic in the kitchen, lotion or perfume applied early in the day on the wrist may be insufficient, but having your child put eucalyptus oil under their nose when they come in the kitchen might make the experience less noxious. Providing a sensory experience that masks or competes with the unpleasant odor can be an effective first step in encouraging them to enter a space that was previously avoided. Giving rewards for entering smelly places and utilizing coping strategies will increase motivation and willingness to participate.

Ten-year-old Sam had been invited to go to the circus again. He had always wanted to see a circus but avoided it due to his sensitivity to smell. Every year Sam would hear about the acrobats, the clowns, the fantastic costumes, and the animals that the other kids saw, and he would feel left out. Sam decided that he really wanted to go this year and told his father that he wanted help facing this task. Sam and his dad practiced using several tools to help him tolerate the unpleasant animal odors. Using the formula for success, they decided to do a practice run with Dad before going with his friends. His formula looked like this: going to the circus with Dad (experience, fun) + chewing cinnamon gum (sensory soothing) + rubbing lavender oil under his nose (sensory soothing) + practicing relaxation skills (coping skills) + using coping statements (coping skills) while at the circus. These targeted tools helped Sam tolerate the smells of the circus, and he was truly able to enjoy himself. While the smells were still annoying to him, he was able to use his tools successfully, which allowed him to feel proud of himself and more confident about future endeavors. His intrinsic reward was going to the circus with his friends, something that he very much wanted to be able to do.

Taste

Children who are under-responsive to taste may be unable to identify foods that have gone bad, might not notice or might seek out strong flavors, or may eat foods that are unappealing to other children (like strong-tasting fish, liver, or very spicy foods). On the other hand, children who are over-responsive to taste may be considered picky eaters, may refuse to eat certain foods, or may gag frequently while eating.

If your child is under-responsive, it may be important to establish rules about what to taste and what not to taste. Some rules might be subtle, such as teaching your child to take cues from others by noticing their behavior, facial reactions, and responses to food. If a friend is making a weird face when you are about to put something in your mouth, you might question whether it is a good idea to eat it. Other rules could be more straightforward: "Never put anything in your mouth that you are not sure is real food" or (if your child is old enough) "read the expiration date on foods before eating them." Children who explore their world through oral stimulation put things in their mouths almost out of habit. Helping your child slow down and identify whether or not something is edible (or appropriate for eating) are key strategies. In addition, having flavored gum or mints available for times when your child is in need of a strong flavor can help get this need met in a more socially appropriate manner. Sometimes children who are under-responsive to taste tend to overeat. If your child struggles with overeating, you may consider limiting portion size and access to food between meals, as well as limiting sugary foods in the home. Chewing gum is a good alternative for children who overeat.

On the other end of the spectrum, working with a child who is a picky eater (over-responsive to taste) can be a creative and fun experience for both you and your child. The goal is to introduce new foods in a way that is fun and exciting. For example, create a picture with food (make it fun), such as cutting an apple and arranging the pieces to look like the shape of a face, filling in the details with raisins for eyebrows, blueberries or blackberries for eyes, and strawberries for lips. You could make a log with ants crawling along it by stuffing a stalk of celery with peanut butter and putting raisins on top. These creative food presentations engage the child's visual senses (sensory soothing) and reduce the stress around eating. The goal is to create a more positive atmosphere (make it fun) that will encourage your child to explore new foods. And having a chart where you can keep track of progress toward prizes for trying novel foods encourages your child to step out of their comfort zone and try things they might previously have avoided.

Children who have an exaggerated gag response due to an oral-tactile sensory over-responsiveness often have limited palates as well. These children are not responding to the taste of the food as much as the texture and how it feels in their mouth. Foods that typically are a challenge for children with these sensory issues are gritty, creamy, mushy, slimy, lumpy, or chewy. To help your child expand their food choices, be sure to start small. Create an Experience Ladder (see chapter 6) that offers foods similar in texture to those foods that are already well tolerated.

Encourage a very small piece or bite of food to start. Choosing foods that taste good but happen to have a different (offensive) texture can also be helpful. In addition, introduce sensory soothing, such as playing their favorite music during meals or having pleasant smells around to offset the novel texture experience. Teach coping skills such as relaxation and coping statements to allow your child to tolerate the unpleasant taste or texture. Be careful not to demand too much too fast. Be patient and allow your child to move slowly up the food Experience Ladder, getting used to the foods at each level before moving to the next level. A common mistake is for parents to insist that their child try a food that is dramatically different in texture, smell, and style from the foods that the they are currently comfortable with. Pushing your child too fast, without sensory soothing or the use of coping strategies, can cause pushback and create resistance to participating or to eating altogether. Rewards for trying new and challenging foods help increase your child's motivation for progress.

Danika is a nine-year-old girl who is a very picky eater. She eats only French fries, fried chicken strips, and pasta with butter. Her parents worked with her to teach her relaxation through deep breathing and confidence by using coping statements such as "I am strong," "I can get used to new foods," "I can eat food that is not one of my favorites," and "I can do this." During the weeks when she was learning and practicing her coping skills, they explored positive sensory soothing and together learned that she likes holding her soft blanket in her lap and loves listening to nature sounds. They talked about how having these things during meals might help her be able to try new foods. Together they made a food Experience Ladder that started with sweet potato fries (similar to French fries) and moved up to sugar snap peas (similar in size and texture), grilled chicken strips, apple strips (cut to look like French fries), and adding a small amount of pasta sauce to her pasta. They began to do the food experiences with the help of sensory soothing and the use of coping skills. With each new food, she earned points that could be used to purchase items at a local store. After six weeks, Danika was able to eat a variety of new foods and was more

willing to try foods that were not even on her Experience Ladder,
because she had developed a foundation of trying and succeeding.

Tactile

Children who are under-responsive to tactile stimuli have a poor sense of touch. They may not respond to pain or may not notice when something is hot, may not notice a scratchy sweater or very cold water, or may investigate tactile sensations in inappropriate ways (touching or rubbing all sorts of objects or people). Children who are over-responders or over-sensitive to touch may avoid being around other people for fear of being touched, have extreme reactions to being dirty, or dislike brushing their teeth, wearing certain clothes, or having their hair brushed.

Again, outlining a set of rules for children who are tactile under-responders may be helpful. For children who are likely to touch things inappropriately, rules might include "assume the stove (or iron or skillet) is hot before touching," "ask a person if it is okay to touch them before doing so," and "do not play with knives (or matches or scissors) without a parent around to help." Children who seek out tactile sensations may benefit from creating their own sensory "pouch" full of interesting items to touch, such as sandpaper, mini koosh balls, smooth stones, swatches of material (like rough wool, satin, terrycloth, and damask), playdough, a feather, a container of slime, pipe cleaners, or yarn. Your child should be encouraged to keep this pouch in their pocket, backpack, or desk at school and to fidget with the items when needing some sensory input. The goal is to keep the nervous system regularly engaged with pleasant sensory experiences and thus reduce the need to seek out other, less appropriate sensory experiences, such as touching other children or objects. If necessary, ask the teacher for permission for your child to use sensory items when listening to a lecture or completing a worksheet.

Kids who over-respond to touch can have extreme reactions to feeling messy or dirty, have limited clothing preferences, and dislike touching things that they perceive to be sticky or wet. Some children even find it difficult to eat a variety of foods due to the residue left on the lips, face, or hands from what they are eating (like peanut butter and jelly from a sandwich or grease and salt from French fries). These children often shy away from any experience that results in the feeling of excess particles or substances on their skin. For these children, making it fun can be beneficial. For example, you might create a home spa experience to encourage exploration of a variety of textures on the face. The spa could start with a facial that includes a facial scrub or mud mask that requires time to dry on the skin. Once the facial is complete and the skin is washed, apply cream to the cheeks, powder to the face, and lip balm to the lips. Another spa experience to try is giving your child a massage with a massage oil that smells good. Give a choice of a light- or deep-tissue massage, how long the massage will last, and what part of the body will be massaged. These experiences allow your child to feel the sensation of substance on the skin and of you touching the skin, while receiving attention from you and the prospect of smooth, soft skin and relaxation as a result. Your child may prefer to be the one *giving* the facial or massage rather than receiving it. This option will be less overwhelming and a good place to begin.

If a spa is not of interest to your child, try creating a kind of Halloween-like party with costumes, makeup, and a house of horrors. Encourage them to try green, blue, or red face paint to dress up as a favorite cartoon character or superhero. The house of horrors might also include touching raw eggs, peeled grapes in a bowl (eyeballs), overcooked slimy and cold noodles (guts), and similar things to make these experiences more fun and, thus, more tolerable.

If your child avoids others because they don't like being touched, a good technique is to create an obstacle course. The obstacle course should start at home, using walls, furniture, family members, and stuffed animals as the obstacles. All family members should be well informed and aware that the goal of the obstacle course is to encourage touch and that your child will be bumping into and touching all items used in the course. Making a game out of this new behavior is designed to motivate your child to engage in and learn to tolerate touch, while having fun at the same time.

For children who find brushing their teeth to be quite unpleasant, create a game of "beat the clock" and see if they can brush longer than the timer. Set the timer for a very short time at first—even just ten seconds the first time—and extend the amount of time every few days. Another fun idea is to play a favorite song while brushing their teeth, requiring that brushing continue until the song has ended—listening to the song is a pleasant distraction from the sensation of the toothbrush.

Brushing hair can also be a challenge for children who are highly reactive to tactile sensations. If this is the case, start by encouraging your child to brush your hair (if this is tolerable to you). Experiment with different brushes and combs, and talk about how each one feels different and about what you like and dislike about each one. If you do not like a particular sensation, model how to experience it even though it is unpleasant. Describe how it feels, but do not react to it or avoid it. Next, encourage your child to allow you to try the same brushes and combs on them and see what feels best. Encourage your child to describe the sensations, both good and bad, without reacting negatively. Children can play barbershop or salon with you or with friends and wash, brush, and style hair in a playful atmosphere (make it fun).

Visual

Children who are under-responsive to things in the visual field are not bothered by bright lights and can appear to be extremely messy. These children may enjoy having items scattered all over the floor, prefer colorful or unmatched clothing, and feel at home in a crowded, messy room. Children who are visually over-responsive may have difficulty looking at items that appear out of place or out of order, they may become overwhelmed when there are bright lights or colorful items in their visual field, and they may have trouble making eye contact.

Under-responsive children often get identified as "messy" and many times will prefer a room that is filled with clutter. These children can be frustrating to parents because they may refuse to clean their rooms or will even create clutter when the room has been cleaned for them. The truth is that these kids like seeing the clutter and mess—it is soothing to their eyes. Ways to help alleviate this situation are to create a visually stimulating environment for them with brightly colored walls, perhaps painted with a mural, or with patterned carpeting or a brightly colored rug. Hang colorful posters on the walls and have striped curtains for the windows— or something else that your child likes. A way to make it fun is to pretend you are interior designers remaking their room to the needs of their senses. Allow your child to select the wall color (or colors), art, and bedding for their room so that it is pleasing to their unique nervous system. Do not worry if your child selects things that you do not like or that do not match. Allow them the freedom to pick items that are pleasing to them, regardless of your personal taste. In all likelihood, you will not like what your child picks, but it is important to respect their choices and honor their nervous system. The goal is to celebrate your child's unique nervous system and to help your child understand their needs and not feel ashamed about them. If your child wants black and white stripes on the wall, help paint them and express how much you love stripes. Your child will pick up on your feelings and reactions, so be careful to show acceptance and support, even when your preferences are quite different. For children who need even more stimulation, create an area where they can be messy. For example, find a large bin that they can dump all of their toys and games into and look at the mess, or if their room is big enough, a small tent that they can crawl into and see the mess all around them. Allow controlled messes that your child can manage and put away when finished.

Over-responsive children do not like messes or visual clutter and react to lots of visual input by avoiding, acting out, or shutting down. If your child over-responds to visual input, it is first important to create a relatively clutter-free atmosphere in the entire home and especially in your child's room. Developing a space that is soothing to your child can, on a daily basis, help them manage their nervous system. Over time, you may introduce new items systematically and one at a time, and give your child a chance to get used to them before adding more. Another idea is to create a game. Place an item in a room where it does not belong or tilt the paintings so that they are not hanging evenly on the wall (experience). The goal is to keep the item in the wrong place or the painting crooked for as long as possible.

Another idea to help with experiencing visual clutter is to designate a "Waldo" item and play a game of "Where's Waldo?" in a more crowded room (make it fun). You can introduce the idea of this visual experience to your child (and practice doing it) by reading one or more of Martin Handford's *Where's Waldo?* books. Younger children may appreciate including their stuffed animal collection in the game. Collect all of the stuffed animals in the house and have a huge family reunion, placing them all on the floor in a room (make it fun). Your child may start by taking attendance. You and your child may create some activities for the family reunion, such as nap time (putting all of the stuffed animals on the bed and even taking a nap with their stuffed animal family members) or having tea time, providing tea and snacks for the family (experience). These are some examples of how to make experiences fun in order to encourage your child to interact with an environment that had previously been overwhelming and therefore avoided.

Some children do not like the way things look when they are not straight (leading to shoes being lined up in the closet, pencils being arranged in a row in the desk, and clothes grouped together by color in drawers and in the closet). If this is the case with your child, try creating an Experience Ladder that slowly mixes things up, but with a twist to make it fun. Have your child make a game out of mismatching the pairs of shoes (but keeping them in a straight row) or arranging the clothes by category (pants, shirts, etc.), instead of by color. Over time, the goal is to help them become more and more comfortable with the look of things not being ordered. Again, the goal is to be flexible, not rigid. Having to have all shoes paired and lined up is a rigid way to approach shoe storage. The goal is not to throw the shoes all over the house and have a huge mess, but for your child to become flexible enough to tolerate them being out of order and in a messy row.

If your child has trouble making eye contact, direct them to notice something about the eyes that is of interest. Together you might create a science experiment collecting data regarding all the people your child speaks with during the week: What is the most common eye color of the people you speak with? How many people have eyebrows that touch in the middle? How many people have long eyelashes? How many people wear glasses? This approach encourages them to look into the eyes of the people with whom they are speaking while gathering information for the experiment. Another trick for children who have difficulty making eye contact is to have them look at people in the middle of their forehead, not in the eyes. The forehead, being blank, is less overwhelming and, while it is not actual eye contact, it gives the other person something closer to eye contact than when your child looks at the floor or to one side. If the person is far enough away, in fact—like the teacher at the front of the classroom—the person might actually think you are making eye contact. Play a game in which your child practices looking at people in the forehead and see whether anyone notices they are not actually looking into their eyes. Give points for every time they are able to fake out another person by looking at their forehead, not at their eyes.

Auditory

Children who are under-responsive to auditory stimuli prefer noise at all times. They may like for the radio to be on at the same time as the television, they may like to listen to music with the volume all the way up to 10 while studying, and they can't stand to be in silence for long periods of time. Those who over-respond to noise often become frightened or overstimulated with loud or surprising sounds. Birthday parties with balloons, thunderstorms, loud flushing toilets, smoke detectors, music concerts, fireworks, and fire alarms can be intolerable for these children. For some children even quiet sounds can create a challenge. For example, some may not be able to filter out hearing items such as a ticking clock, the humming of a computer, or another child clicking a pen in school.

For those who are under-responsive to noise, employing rules is key: "Only one piece of equipment (television, radio, stereo) on at a time" or "Listen to music with the volume no higher than 7 in a public area of the house." Allow your child to listen to louder volumes (within reason) in the privacy of their bedroom or while wearing headphones to be respectful toward family or friends. Sometimes children with poor auditory detection speak loudly and cannot perceive how loud they are speaking. If this is the case for your child, help them monitor their voice volume regularly. Initially, have a subtle hand gesture to indicate that their voice is too loud (perhaps a subtle finger pointing to the ear or an open hand pushing in a downward direction). After your child has gotten used to these signals, if they still have difficulty recognizing their own voice volume, try speaking in a softer tone, to give a subtle hint. Over time, they should begin to self-regulate their volume, but this is indeed a process.

Over-responsive children (those who dislike loud noise) benefit greatly from learning coping skills such as using headphones, practicing relaxation training, or doing deep breathing to cope when loud noises are present and cannot be avoided. Together, create an Experience Ladder by searching the internet for sounds that are increasingly uncomfortable to hear. Instruct your child to use headphones to quiet noise at the lower levels of the ladder. While using headphones, practice relaxation skills to help move up the ladder of sounds. During the first few experiences, the sound should be something pleasant (like gentle music or birds singing), and it may be barely audible, while further up the ladder the volume increases and the sounds are more unpleasant (such as traffic noises, a loud crowd of people, and an ambulance siren). Relaxation, deep breathing, and coping statements should all be used during experience work. Each time your child participates, give them a reward for the hard work.

As confidence grows and the ability to tolerate sounds increases, encourage them to make their own playlist of sounds. If subtle background noise is the problem, practice listening to a clock ticking or a sound machine with white noise. Use strategies such as deep breathing, relaxation, counting the ticks, imagining that the white noise is the wind, dancing to the sound of static, or other creative approaches that distract from negative emotions or behaviors. Instead of trying to not hear the noise, allow the noise to be there and, perhaps, imagine that it is something else.

When mealtime noises (chewing and swallowing) are intolerable, you may start by pretending that you are in a restaurant that plays loud music. While in your dining room, turn up the music during a meal and encourage your child to practice coping statements, deep breathing, and using a sensory-soothing item such as a cozy blanket on their lap during meals. Over time, reduce the sound of the music so that the noises of chewing and swallowing are more audible. You may experiment with other types of music as well, ultimately playing some kind of especially gentle classical music. Who knows—maybe your whole family will prefer listening to soft music during meals.

The Near Senses

You may remember from chapter 2 that the near senses are the internal senses, the ones that evaluate internal states, such as feeling hungry (interoceptive), sensing movement (vestibular), and experiencing body position and space (proprioceptive). The near senses are a bit more elusive than the far senses, which are more obvious and things that we all can easily relate to. Problems with regulation of the near senses are a bit more difficult to identify because they can be subtle and hard to detect.

Interoceptive

Children who under-respond to their internal states have difficulty recognizing these states at all and are not able to tell when they are hungry, thirsty, hot or cold, excited, need to use the restroom, and so forth. These children will not eat spontaneously unless prompted, will wear shorts in a snowstorm, and frequently have bathroom accidents. Those who have an over-responsive system tend to dislike those feelings and have difficulty tolerating sensations such as a fast heartbeat, needing to use the restroom, actually using the restroom, or feeling hot, cold, hungry, or thirsty. These children will eat or drink too much to avoid hunger or thirst, will avoid moving their bowels because the feeling of it is unpleasant, will avoid exercise that makes their heart beat quickly, and will avoid large temperature changes.

Many of these children, on both sides of the spectrum, benefit from a firm daily schedule, which may be thought of as an experience. Important daily events such as meals, snacks, bathroom use, and bedtime can be set into a reliable routine. Set a reasonable portion size for snacks and meals, particularly when your child is young. In this way, you are helping your child learn to make appropriate decisions regarding when and how much to eat and drink. The same is true for elimination—set a daily schedule for using the restroom. Every morning your child should sit on the toilet for at least twenty minutes to try to have a bowel movement. Children who are dysregulated in this area either do not recognize the need to go to the bathroom or do not like the feeling of it and avoid it as much as possible. Setting a regular schedule helps them feel that going to the bathroom is predictable (avoiding accidents later in the day) and that it is just a regular part of the day.

Sensory interventions during bathroom time can be helpful. Encourage your child to play with interesting toys, use a head massager, play games on a tablet, listen to music, and employ coping skills such as relaxation, coping statements, and deep breathing to help them tolerate this uncomfortable situation and experience success. Having a schedule also helps organize the environment and expectations, as well as training the nervous system to expect needing to go to the bathroom every day. Schedules for urination can help avoid accidents as well. Set a schedule for school that requires a trip to the restroom at two-hour intervals, as well as right after school, to ensure frequent opportunities to urinate.

For children who do not like a fast heartbeat, use skills such as relaxation training after doing jumping jacks to help your child learn to tolerate the internal senses and also be able to exert some control over these uncomfortable feelings. For those who fail to recognize hunger or thirst, a daily schedule also works for eating meals and drinking fluids. Having a routine that is fairly predictable each day helps set expectations and encourages them to rely on the schedule rather than unreliable internal states to determine when it is time to eat or drink. Rewards for following the schedule both at home and at school can encourage motivation and commitment to the process.

Vestibular

Children who are under-responsive to the vestibular sense crave movement and may spin, rock, run, and bounce from place to place with little regard to appropriateness or safety. These children seem to be in constant motion. By contrast, children who are over-responsive to movement may find movement unpleasant, therefore places like playgrounds and amusement parks might be disliked or avoided. These children often dislike climbing, swinging, sliding, riding in a car, and even swimming.

If your child craves movement, you will need to provide many appropriate opportunities for them to engage in active movement on a daily basis. Having a small trampoline in their bedroom is helpful to provide access to movement in a safe way. Participating in sports and outdoor activities can also help get this need for movement met. Sitting on an exercise ball or wiggle cushion instead of a chair at the dinner table or their desk can help your child get much needed movement, even while seated. Playing with a squishy toy, rubbing a smooth stone, or chewing gum might not feel like much movement, but these subtle movements can be enough to allow your child to sit still in environments where movement is not appropriate, like houses of worship, classrooms, or movie theaters.

For vestibular over-responsive children, use the Experience Ladder to help them systematically engage in movement. Activities such as swinging on a swing set, with increasing intensity (experience), while listening to a favorite song or counting the number of pushes (sensory soothing, make it fun) to alleviate some of the discomfort from movement, is also a good way to get started. Once a child is more confident and comfortable with movement, activities on the ladder such as joining a gymnastics class or soccer or swimming lessons are great, as these activities build on basic skills such as walking in a straight line on a mat and then move to summersaults or gross motor movement like running or moving arms through water. Talk to your child about what sport or activity they enjoy watching and would like to play and use that as a goal to work toward when your child is working through early rungs on the Experience Ladder. You might even add some soccer or swimming skills to those early rungs, like kicking a ball in the backyard or swinging the arms in the movement of swimming. Children who are over-responsive to movement almost always have a tendency toward carsickness. Be sure to have pleasant sensory input (smells, sounds, textures, visuals) for long or windy car rides to help combat the nausea that accompanies any movement associated with car travel.

Proprioceptive

Children who have challenges with the proprioceptive sense have difficulty knowing where their body is in relation to other objects. They can appear rigid, tense, and inflexible, or they may seem awkward as they bump into objects, have poor coordination, and are challenged playing sports such as football, basketball, volleyball, and tennis. Taking a yoga or stretching class is an ideal way for sensory-dysregulated children to gain experience in movement. These classes can help your child learn how it feels to stretch their bodies, loosen rigid postures, and increase flexibility. In addition, a class atmosphere encourages fun, socialization, and comradery while challenging the proprioceptive sense. If spatial orientation is hard for your child, be careful not to push them into a sport that will be too difficult, such as football, baseball, or soccer, at too young of an age. More appropriate sports, such as karate, gymnastics, track, dance, or yoga, should be explored first, to increase body awareness while encouraging movement. Other, more challenging sports can be introduced later, once proprioceptive skills have been built and tolerance for this type of movement is established.

Conclusion

This is by no means an exhaustive list of techniques that might be used when helping your child to regulate their sensory system—rather, it is a starting point. These ideas are suggestions for helping your child successfully regulate their nervous system, with the assistance of sensory soothing, coping skills, making it fun, and using rewards to encourage participation. Be careful not to try to work on too many things at once. Talk to your child about what areas bother them the most and what areas would be the most helpful to work through first. Try working on one area at a time and, if needed, shift to another area if one is not working or if you get too much pushback from your child. Take your time and go slowly, with patience and encouragement. If one of the areas is hard for you as well, be willing to work on it at the same time that your child works on their issue. In some cases, when a child is just too opposed to making change, a referral to an occupational therapist is a good first step, as these professionals are trained to help children address sensory-based issues. However, the strategies listed here are worth trying at home, because they can be practiced daily and because you spend the majority of time with your child and know them best. The next chapter will discuss the critical role that you as a parent play when helping your child learn successful sensory regulation.

CHAPTER 8

The Challenging Child in Context
How to Support Your Child and Strengthen Your Relationship

Because you spend the majority of time with your child, you may have noticed that the preponderance of problems with their behavior occurs when they are with you. This can be quite frustrating. Therefore, your interactions with your child are the most important avenue for helping your child achieve sensory regulation, which will improve their behavior, family dynamics, and ultimately long-term harmonious family functioning. Unaddressed, difficult behaviors such as crying, refusing to participate, oppositional behavior, inappropriate sensory seeking, and avoidance of activities can cause a tremendous amount of tension and frustration, not only for you, as parents, but also for the entire family. This chapter presents an overview of your role in supporting your child, provides specific tools for positive parenting, and guides you on how to avoid making common parenting mistakes. In summary, we want to help you be the most effective parent possible.

Accommodating Problematic Behaviors

Accommodation is the process of adapting or adjusting to your child's behavior. For example, I might accommodate my child who asks for help on his math homework when I had planned to go to the movies with my friend. Instead of going to the movie, I choose to help him by accommodating his request. Accommodation is something we do to be helpful.

However, sometimes we, as parents, accommodate behaviors that we should not accommodate, such as when your child screams at the store that they want a lollipop and you know that you should not buy it, but they scream so much that you give in just to make them be quiet.

Why do parents accommodate a child's seemingly poor behavior, even when they know it is not the right thing to do? Typically, parents respond to a child's distress with an attempt to relieve that distress—or to relieve their *own* distress caused by the child screaming in the middle of the store! When a child is perceived to be suffering, parents can feel anxious or frustrated and want to do something to make the child feel better. Well-meaning parents often fall prey to their own anxiety or frustration and respond to their child's behavior by accommodating (doing exactly what the child wants). For example, if a child is terrified of dogs, their mother might make sure that they never have to interact with a dog by asking friends and family members to remove dogs from the house when they visit, by avoiding places where dogs might be present, and by never owning a dog. In a way, parents may feel like relieving distress is part of their job as a good parent, while *not* helping would seem like a failure on their part to help solve a problem. They are just trying to be helpful, right?

There are many common examples of other ways parents accommodate childhood fears or sensory regulation issues:

- Sleeping with their child (or allowing the child to sleep in the parent's bed) to ensure a good night's sleep and soothe anxieties.

- Eliminating chores and responsibilities so as not to add too much stress for the child.

- Allowing their anxious child to stay home from school for days or weeks to avoid the possibility of being upset at school.

- Being unwilling to set appropriate limits with a child due to a desire to keep the peace.

- Completing tasks for children (homework, projects, chores) to shield them from stress.

- Failing to give consequences for inappropriate behavior for fear that symptoms may worsen.

Unfortunately, these parenting behaviors do the opposite of what you ultimately want for your child, which is for them to be happy and free from stress. Allowing your child to somehow benefit from behaving anxiously actually reinforces the anxious behavior. Think about a child who is afraid to go to bed at night because it is dark (visual) and very quiet (auditory). Their parents might accommodate the child's anxiety by allowing them to sleep in their bed to alleviate the fear of the quiet darkness and to allow them to get some good sleep. Unfortunately, while the child's anxiety might be reduced for the moment, a much bigger problem has just been created. Now the child relies on the comfort of sleeping in the parents' bed and may come to resist sleeping in their own bed. What might have seemed like a solution in the moment can turn into a more complex problem in the long run.

A healthier approach, one that uses the *tolerance for the sensory triggers formula,* is to help them become more self-sufficient by altering their bedroom environment to be more soothing and favorable to them. First, the parents might allow them to have a night-light or to keep a lamp on (sensory soothing—visual) while they sleep in their own room (experience). Second, parents might add white noise or soft music to reduce the sensation of silence (sensory soothing—auditory). Third, super soft blankets might be added, and smells, colors, or other sensory-soothing items that might be pleasing to them (sensory soothing—tactile). It is important for the parents to allow their child to choose what their nervous system likes, not to base choices on what they like. Fourth, the parents might teach them to use coping statements like "I am safe" and "I can do this" or to practice deep breathing and relaxation skills (coping skills) while lying in bed. Finally, they might give a reward (make it fun) for going to bed in their own bed *and* for waking up in their own bed. Rewards might be things like points or stickers that could add up to tangible rewards. For example, if they are able to earn ten points, they might earn a trip to their favorite store for a small toy or might get to have a friend spend the night.

It is important for you to recognize any potential accommodating behaviors and to address them directly. Often this requires you, as parents, to be willing to tolerate your own frustration and anxiety in the process. It is hard to watch your child suffer. We have all been there and know how awful it can feel. Let's go back to the example of the child who is afraid to sleep in their room in the dark and quiet. In the moment, it may seem better to give in, to allow them to sleep with their parents to reduce the child's distress. However, as we now know, this is actually reinforcing the anxiety and the inability to sleep on their own in their own room. It also encourages the child's dependence on their parents instead of fostering self-reliance and a sense of self-efficacy in solving problems. The child will develop a belief that they must sleep in their parents' room to feel safe and comfortable.

One might think that this is a reasonable solution, but ironically, this accommodation can feel bad to a child. They may feel unable or poorly equipped to manage things on their own, which can diminish self-confidence. By doing the hard work now and learning to sleep in their own room successfully, they will be more able to face hard things later in life. This work is hard for both you and your child! Through this work your child will be facing their fears, and you will need to manage your own feelings about seeing your child's discomfort as they figure things out. Avoiding the hard work now only postpones the inevitable. Your child eventually has to face whatever the feared task might be, potentially when they are older and not able to benefit from your support. Remember to be firm but loving, to encourage them to face the challenge, and to celebrate all victories, no matter how big or small.

Take a Moment: Think about a time when you had to do something that was hard. Maybe you had to face a fear or meet a challenge that you would have preferred to avoid. How did you do it? What helped you be successful in facing this challenge? Most importantly, what did you learn from facing this challenge? How did facing the challenge and not avoiding it help you the next time you had to face a challenge? Now, think about some coping statements that you can use for yourself when you are facing a difficult challenge with your child. When your child is having a hard moment, and you feel inclined to give in, what can you do to help you stay strong in that moment? What can you say to yourself that will remind you that supporting your child to have this experience is actually the better choice than giving in? What words would help you be strong in those moments when you want to give in and rescue your child from their fear or anxiety? Write these words down in a place where you can access them in difficult situations—on a sticky note on the refrigerator, for instance, or take a photo of that sticky note and make the photo the wallpaper on your phone. Read these words regularly so that you are prepared when you need them. Practice taking care of yourself and telling yourself these words in times of stress.

Your role as a parent is that of supporter and advocate, not as rescuer and appeaser. During this process, you will likely make changes in your approach to parenting, such as setting firmer limits, reducing or discontinuing accommodating behaviors, or encouraging your child to engage in challenging behaviors that were previously avoided, which are all hard to do! These changes to parental behaviors often do not feel good or soothing to a child, and you must be prepared for your child's reaction of resistance, frustration, anger, or increased anxiety. Remember that you are a barometer for your child's emotions. If you stay calm, your child will eventually become calm. If you escalate your frustration, anger, or anxiety, so will your child. Remember to breathe and use your own coping statements. Remind yourself that these steps are for the best and that, in the long run, they will help your child much more than giving in would. And remember that you are being a better parent by encouraging your child to face their fear or discomfort.

Remember Lucy from chapter 3? Lucy does not like the fire alarms at school and, due to her frightened reaction to the alarm, her parents decided to find out the alarm schedule so that future alarms could be easily avoided by keeping her home. This accommodation could lead to Lucy not wanting to go to school at all due to a fear of an unplanned alarm happening. It also gives her the message that she can't handle a fire drill. The approach that employs tolerance for the sensory triggers formula would be to allow her to wear noise-canceling headphones during an alarm (coping skill), practicing listening to alarms on the internet at louder and louder volumes until she can tolerate them (experience), allowing her to have a friend by her side during alarms giving her support and encouragement (make it fun), teaching her coping statements such as "I can stand this for five minutes—that is as long as it will last!" and giving her rewards for staying at school on days when there is an alarm scheduled (make it fun). Support and encouragement are the keys here. In the beginning, she may not want to participate, but with a well-designed reward system, support, and encouragement, she will get on board and experience success. Experiencing success, even small victories, will lead to improved confidence and willingness to face uncomfortable situations in the future.

Avoid Punishment

The opposite of accommodation is punishment, which is defined as a negative event that follows a behavior. Punishment can be verbal, physical, or tangible (taking away a toy or sending a child to their room). Oftentimes parents may take a less sympathetic approach and, in an attempt to correct a behavior, will discipline a child who is truly suffering and struggling with sensory regulation. In an attempt to be good parents, they will:

- try to insist on full participation by yelling and shaming a child who is avoiding something (food, places, or activities);

- eliminate all sources of entertainment, including television, phone, computer, or outings with friends, in order to "motivate" the child into behaving better; or

- force their child to do things that they are avoiding, which is more likely to cause oppositional behavior or even depression.

Tyler (from chapter 4) could not stand the feeling of both feet on the ground, so he would hop around on one foot. Before seeking therapy, his parents were extremely frustrated and thought he was simply acting up. They were also a bit embarrassed by his strange behavior and would correct him repeatedly in public. Despite Tyler's repeated requests to his parents to not call him out in public, they continued to do so as they thought it would lead to enough embarrassment for him that he would eventually stop. They also gave the consequence of "no playing with friends" if he did not walk using both feet, something that was very hard for him to do. Tyler became ashamed of himself and how his body felt, and he began to believe that something was wrong with him. He started to avoid walking around his parents and eventually other people and developed a deep sense of shame about his internal sensory world.

Many times parents are behaving the way their parents did with them, or they are trying to help their children by presenting strict expectations and consequences for what they deem to be misbehavior. We are all doing our best to try to help our children function and be successful. However, punishing a child for something that they cannot help and is beyond their control is really not fair. It only causes confusion and pain for the child.

The approaches of accommodation and punishment are equally ineffective and lead to children feeling more anxious, depressed, and misunderstood when they are chastised or made fun of for something that they cannot control. Imagine that you are on an airplane flying at thirty thousand feet, and the flight attendant announces over the intercom that the passengers will all have to jump out of the plane without parachutes. Everyone on the plane is lining up and preparing to jump. You are terrified and start to panic. You are pleading with the attendant and others to *not have to do this*. You might feel confused about why no one else is having a problem with this and why they are all jumping out of the plane. You might find yourself hiding in the bathroom or clinging to a seat for your life, refusing to approach the plane door. Your behavior might seem bizarre to the other people, who do not see a problem with jumping out.

While this example may seem strange to you, it may help you see how terrifying it feels for a child who has a problem with nervous system regulation to be asked to do something that goes against their nervous system. It feels catastrophic, possibly even life threatening, igniting the sympathetic nervous system response of fight, flight, or freeze. Now imagine that you are punished for not jumping; you are made fun of and told that you are in trouble for not doing as you are told. This would be confusing. You would think, *Why am I in trouble for doing something that is so obviously correct?* Hopefully this example demonstrates how a child feels when asked to do something that is in direct conflict with their nervous system, and how the nervous system responds with resistance, fear, and avoidance.

Punishment for behaviors that are rooted in sensory regulation issues is never the answer and does not lead to positive behavior change. Punishment should be reserved for acting out behaviors that are willful and within a child's direct control. In cases of willful disobedience, punishment should be logical (it should fit the crime and not be excessive) and should be brief. Most importantly, when possible, expectations should be spelled out ahead of time with the consequences clearly explained. When a child has nervous system regulation problems and reacts to sensory triggers in nontraditional ways, you must be careful not to punish those responses. Understanding your child and their nervous system is crucial in understanding their behavior. Know which behaviors are the result of sensory sensitivities and which are simply acts of willful defiance or testing the limits. Punishing a child for something that is not under their control is both confusing and upsetting.

Back to the example of Tyler, who had a hard time putting both feet on the ground at the same time. Once his parents were told that Tyler's behavior was due to sensory issues beyond his control, they stopped demanding compliance and started using a different approach. Using the tolerance for sensory triggers formula, they learned that he absolutely loved country music and allowed him to play his favorite county artists on his headphones (sensory soothing—auditory). He also was calmed by the smell of lavender and the texture of satin and soft fabrics (sensory soothing smell and touch). His parents bought him some lavender essential oil to put under his nose (sensory soothing—smell) and some thick, soft socks (sensory soothing—touch) to wear around the house to practice walking with both feet touching the ground. Using these additional sensory soothing tools, he was able to walk without hopping for short periods of time. His parents rewarded him for walking longer and longer distances without hopping. One night the whole family had a "dance party" where they played different types of music, including his favorite country songs, and all family members danced (make it fun). The party was a fun way to encourage movement with feet and touching the ground in a different way (dancing) that helped him get more comfortable with more and more foot touch.

When developing an approach to facing sensory sensations that are difficult, it is important to be positive and encourage your child to try things that are hard for them to do. Using phrases like "I know you can do it" and "start small and add on" help your child turn toward difficult sensory situations, and it gives them the opportunity to experience success. Setting up a reinforcement and reward schedule, rather than punishment, is imperative when working with children who have problems with sensory regulation. You will provide your child with the support and encouragement needed to be successful in facing their fears.

The role for any parent changes dramatically from one developmental stage to the next. When sensory regulation leads to disruptive, anxious, or age-inappropriate behaviors, your level of involvement changes even more dramatically. The following section describes typical functioning for each stage of childhood development and how sensory regulation can impact the family system, as well as how you can manage these issues at each developmental stage. Some of these may describe developmental stages that are younger or older than your child at this time; however, we find it important for you to reflect back on earlier phases of life to better understand what was happening with your child at that stage and to look forward to the future and be able to anticipate milestones and tasks that may lay ahead.

Sensory Dysregulation Across Developmental Stages

Developmental Stage: Birth to Two Years

It is helpful to understand the tasks children face at each developmental stage before beginning to understand a child with sensory regulation issues. Although it is highly likely that your child is older than two years old, we believe it is important for you to understand what problems with sensory regulation look like in a very young child so that you can understand why your child may have behaved the way they did early on, as well as how early childhood behavior can impact the relationship you have with your child. If the relationship has been impacted, it is not too late to mend things in the present. It is never too late to work on developing a loving relationship with your child, no matter what age.

The developmental experience for babies (from birth to age two) includes an inability to communicate needs; a restricted environment (stays in a crib); an inability to identify or independently meet needs for food, rest, stimulation, or mobility; and a limited means of coping. Problems with sensory regulation at this early developmental stage can undermine the confidence of parents, because they feel as if they cannot effectively meet the most basic needs of their child. Specifically, these babies are not able to be soothed, seem inconsolable, are in constant discomfort, cry incessantly, and appear to be unhappy most of the time, despite great efforts from parents to soothe and comfort them. In addition, parents may get subtle or overt messages from their parents and friends that they are doing something wrong to cause the distress. Does any of this sound familiar?

Problems with sensory regulation in a very young child can greatly impact parents and can interrupt the establishment of a daily routine, disrupt family life, and sometimes cause marital discord. Not understanding why a child is unhappy and not being able to console them can be extremely difficult and stressful for parents and families. Understanding that sensory issues are the underlying cause, not poor parenting, provides an excellent opportunity to improve your coping (not blaming yourself), gain a better understanding of the source of your child's distress, and learn new, unconventional ways to soothe your child and relieve them of discomfort, thus helping them eventually learn to soothe themself. There are many ways to soothe a dysregulated, inconsolable child:

- Tight swaddling and less human touch can provide a nice break from stimulation.

- Placing the child in a car seat on top of a dryer that is turned on (with supervision). This provides sensory vibrations that some children find comforting.

- Leaving a noise machine or the vacuum cleaner turned on near the child. The constant humming sound can be soothing to some.

- Feeding with a bottle instead of a breast if they are unwilling to nurse.

- Strapping the child into a wearable carrier while walking around the house completing tasks or while running errands. The warmth and movement of the parent can be soothing to the child.

At this developmental stage, the most important task for parents is to learn to soothe their child without feeling at fault. Even babies pick up on parental frustration and insecurity and respond with the same. Know that it is *not your fault* that your child is hard to settle and keep searching for ways to calm their nervous system. You may need to ask for help in times of difficulty. Having a family member come over to give you a break or to help you interact with your baby may be exactly what is needed with children this young.

Developmental Stage: Two to Five Years

The developmental stage for toddlers and preschool-aged children includes gaining certain skills: developing verbal skills; expanding their environment through walking and sleeping in a regular bed; communicating needs for food, rest, and stimulation; and developing some coping skills. Without assistance, babies who have sensory regulation issues typically grow into toddlers who suffer from those problems and can continue to disrupt family life. Toddlers who are over-responders will have meltdowns and temper tantrums, will bite others, and may be unwilling to participate in age-appropriate activities, while under-responders may seek soothing in unconventional ways by touching, eating, licking, and smelling objects inappropriately. Grandparents, friends, and even strangers can be eager to offer parenting advice, often implying that your child is misbehaving due to poor parenting. These well-meaning suggestions can undermine a parent's already fragile confidence, leading parents to feel ineffective at managing their own children.

With babies from birth to age two, a parent may feel completely helpless and confused about why their child is inconsolable, but during the toddler years, children begin to be able to verbalize their discomfort. At this point, parents are also somewhat aware of what is bothering them, but oftentimes they are mistaken about why it is a problem for the child. In other words, a child might be able to say "I hate hairbrushes!" but they are not able to explain their feelings accurately: "It feels like you are stabbing my scalp with toothpicks when you brush my hair, and I cannot stand the pain!" For this reason, avoidant or resistant behavior at this age can get classified as "terrible twos" or "oppositional" when, in fact, it may have a sensory genesis.

It is helpful to do experiments with your toddler to see what works to make specific experiences more tolerable. For example, trying a soft hairbrush, using lots of conditioner in the hair while washing, and playing soft music while brushing hair might all help. You will not know what works and what does not work until you try different experiments to see what your child can and cannot tolerate. Experiments can also be helpful in restoring a sense of confidence and competence in parents of young children. Simply understanding that it is not your fault can help you stay calm, try sensory experiments, and move toward responding differently. You can express that understanding as coping statements: *It is not my fault. My child has some differences that are causing these disturbances in behavior.*

Very young children are highly reliant on their parents to get even their most basic needs met. You determine when and what to eat, what to wear, when to sleep, and in what type of activities to participate. The world of the young child largely revolves around you and the environment that you create. Therefore, at this stage of development, you are the most important part of managing your child's environment and experience, thus helping your child learn skills to be able to tolerate specific sensory situations. Focus on making the environment soothing, calm, structured, and predictable to increase a sense of calm and harmony within the home.

Developmental Stage: Five to Twelve Years

Typical development for this age includes increasing contact with the outside world, beyond the family. Children begin to forge their own relationships with peers and with non-family adults, like teachers and coaches and the parents of friends. This stage is also referred to as the "age of industry" because children are acquiring academic, athletic, musical, and social skills. They begin to compare themselves to others academically, socially, and economically. They are learning a multitude of things on a daily basis. Remember that some of what they are learning has to do with their body's responses to different sensory stimuli. They might learn "I hate car rides" (due to nausea from motion sickness) or "I only eat soft foods" (due to a texture preference for soft rather than hard foods) or "I can't stand birthday parties" (due to an over-response to noise, smell, and visual stimulation). Coincidently, this developmental stage is also the age of onset for troubles with learning differences, ADHD, Tourette syndrome, anxiety disorders, and increased stress due to expectations from school, sports, and family.

When children in this stage of development have sensory regulation issues, their behavior is often marked by noncompliance, frequent tantrums, or abrupt meltdowns. These and other avoidant behaviors (avoidance of loud parties and of going to the beach or an amusement park) can impact peer relationships, academics, and relationships with important adults, such as teachers. Teachers may also contact you with concerns regarding your child's behavior—if your child is unwilling to go outside for recess, has difficulty completing basic work assignments for fear of making a mistake, or is exhibiting oppositional, rigid behavior.

At this age, we recommend that you and your child become a team. Teach your child what you have learned through reading this book. Talk daily about their sensory experience so that you understand fully and clearly the things that they like and do not like and how it all affects their behavior. Learning about the nervous system and how this sensitive system interacts with behavior can help you both better understand their sensory experience and their needs, and encourages an alliance between you and your child.

As a team, you can inform other adults—grandparents, teachers, family friends, or babysitters—about what type of environment and sensory experiences are soothing and helpful, and which ones are not. Explain to other people in your child's life about their nervous system and what they like and do not like. Be matter-of-fact about your explanation and be careful not to use excuses or judgment when describing the situation. The most important part of being a team with your child is to be supportive and have their back.

Being proactive and recognizing and then addressing situations that might be difficult for your child is also an important part of being a team member. Depending on where you and your child are in the process of learning sensory regulation, you may deal with situations a bit differently. For example, if your child is working on their Experience Ladder for facing loud noises, you might encourage them to enter the loud restaurant that happens to be having a big party. You might frame this as an opportunity to move up the ladder, even though it was not planned. Later in the week, you might encounter an unexpected situation with your child that involves a strong smell. Because your child has not started working on that Experience Ladder, you might say, "Hey, I know that this might be hard for you and that we aren't working on this yet. I completely respect it if you don't want to go here this time because it might smell bad to you. What do you think?" Then you would take your child's lead on whether or not to enter the smelly place.

Developmental Stage: Twelve to Seventeen Years

Adolescence is typically a tumultuous stage for any child and their family. This stage includes harder academic tasks, increasing academic demands, and beginning to plan for the future. Social tasks entail separating from the family, increased independence, and asking *Who am I?* Adolescents start to value their peers' opinions above those of the family. Teenagers emerge as sexual beings, beginning to identify sexual orientation and making decisions about becoming sexually active. More than anything, adolescence is a time for rebellion and conflict with parents, ranging from mild resistance to severe acting out. And, believe it or not, all of this is for adolescents with rather "normal" nervous systems!

When problems with sensory regulation are present and not recognized prior to adolescence, behavioral responses to difficult sensory experiences can become extreme and may significantly impair academic, social, and family functioning. In addition, these adolescents have typically suffered for years without understanding why they feel the way they do. Many times these young adults feel misunderstood, different from their peers, and isolated in their experience. Years of well-practiced habits make behavior change more difficult, although it is still possible. In addition, parents may have engaged in years of reacting with frustration, accommodation, or punishment. Some might have simply given up thinking that things can change with regard to their child's behavior. Sometimes, just understanding the adolescent's nervous system and why they have been avoiding and resisting for so many years can be an aha moment that opens the door to healing.

Reading this book and doing the Take a Moment exercises to better understand your child's sensory experience and behavior is perhaps the most powerful intervention at this stage, because it answers so many previously unanswered questions. Typical parent reactions to gaining this information can be that of relief (that you finally understand your child), disbelief (that something physiological can explain what you always assumed to be willful or bad behavior), or guilt (that you have so profoundly misunderstood and blamed your child for all of these years). Adolescents tend to react with relief (that they are finally understood), anger (at you for not having learned this earlier), or "I told you so" reactions toward you. Understand that all of this is normal and expected. When talking to your adolescent about sensory issues, explain that you did not understand, that you misjudged their behavior, and that together you will both work toward healing. If you have behaved under misguided beliefs in the past, tell them that you are sorry and that you will do better in the future. Together you can work toward healing and better relationships in the future.

Parenting at Every Stage of Development

It is important to be informed about normal childhood development and how anxiety and problems with sensory regulation can impact behavior. We hope you have gained some insight into your child from reading about the early stages of development. Your involvement in helping your child varies depending upon your child's age and developmental stage. However, it is important to know that no matter what age your child is, you can benefit from being reminded of certain basic parenting principles—for example, any attention can be reinforcing (meaning that it can cause poor behavior to happen more). When a child is engaging in a problematic behavior, and their parent yells, gets upset, talks to them, or comforts them, the dysfunctional behavior may be reinforced. So we all have to be careful how we respond to our child's behavior, good and bad.

Focus on the Relationship

What decades of research has shown us is that the most important thing in a child's life is the relationship they have with their primary care-takers, who are usually their parents. Nothing is worth putting the relationship you have with your child at risk for becoming damaged. At the end of the day, you want your child to feel loved, accepted, and understood. Even if you have not understood your child and their sensory difficulties in the past, it is not too late to start. Relationships can heal, even after damage has taken place. If this is the case in your relationship, take time to heal the relationship by talking with your child, explaining why you did not understand their behavior, apologizing for any past reactions you may have had because of your misunderstanding, and telling them that you love them unconditionally. Saying "I'm sorry" also models for your child the appropriate thing to do when you hurt another person; it makes them more likely to apologize for their wrongdoings in the future.

Notice the Positive

A good rule of thumb at any age of a child's life is to catch them being good! Reinforce the behavior that you want to see more of. Most parents inadvertently pay more attention to their child's unwanted behaviors and ignore desirable behaviors. This is probably because we are trying to be helpful and to correct what is *not* going right rather than celebrating what *is* going well. However, focusing on the negative results in the exact opposite of what we all hope to accomplish. Parents end up reinforcing those dysfunctional behaviors, and the new and preferred behaviors go unrewarded. It is important to notice, comment on, and reward any positive behavior that you see if you want to see it again.

Sometimes parents will say, "Why should I reward something that they should be doing anyway, like picking up their dirty clothes?" The answer is: *If you want to see a behavior again, praise them for it.* If your child has never picked up their dirty clothes off the floor (and you have reminded them ten thousand times to do so), when they do it, make sure to say,

"Great job picking up your clothes!" It may seem like a silly thing to do, because that is simply an expectation of living in the household, but you will need to do it if you want that behavior to continue. Not noticing sends the message that you really don't care whether they do or don't pick up their clothes or that it did not matter enough for you to notice. If it goes unnoticed, it will likely go away.

Ignore the Negative

The opposite is true for dysfunctional behaviors. If you have been inadvertently paying attention to problem behaviors, try ignoring them. This is helpful at any age of a child's life. If your six-year-old pours their milk on the floor, then looks at you to see your reaction, simply say, "Oops! That was a mistake. Here is a cloth so you can clean it up." If your fourteen-year-old screams that they will not pick up their clothes, simply walk away. You will give a consequence in time, but by disengaging in that conflict or battle you are not giving energy to that behavior. Eventually, that behavior will extinguish. Think about it this way: when you are tending a garden, you want to feed, fertilize, and nurture the plants that you want to grow, not the weeds. By paying attention to the problem behaviors, you are feeding the weeds, not the beautiful flowers that you want to fill your garden. If you are not careful, the weeds will overtake the garden and make it harder for the beautiful plants to thrive and grow.

Expect Things to Get Worse Before They Get Better

One last important behavioral principle to understand when trying to change a child's behavior is the extinction burst. People believe that if they ignore a behavior, it will immediately go away. This is not true. Initially, there is an increase or burst of the behavior before it goes away or becomes extinct. Expect this burst or increase. Do not become discouraged, as things *will* improve with time and patience. Imagine that the weeds will make a last-ditch effort to overtake the garden before dying off. Know that this overgrowth of weeds is only temporary and that they will die off if you are able to stay the course of ignoring and not feeding them. You must be prepared for and anticipate this phenomenon if you are to be successful using the technique of ignoring.

The Importance of Empathy and Relating to Your Child

Empathy is the ability to put yourself in another person's shoes to attempt to understand their experience. As parents, we must imagine what it feels like to be in our child's shoes to have their experiences. When we are in a state of empathy, we are able to establish a more meaningful connection with another person, causing that person to feel understood and validated. Unless your child is adopted (and therefore not your biological child), it is almost always the case that either you or your spouse also experienced some sensory regulation problems while growing up. If you did not have these issues as a child, but your spouse did, talk to your spouse to better learn what it felt like and how they interacted with the world, given their nervous system irregularities. If you did experience sensory regulation issues as a child, it is helpful early on to explore your understanding of your own nervous system to get a clearer understanding of what your child is dealing with. Examine your own nervous system's likes and dislikes or ask your parents about your own history as a child to better understand how your sensory system affected your behavior. Parents may not have understood these behaviors at that time, but we do understand them now. Normalizing sensory experiences for your child by providing personal experience either in the past or even in the present is validating for your child—it shows them that you get it, that you understand their world.

Avoid Shame

There is a huge difference between sending the message that your child *made a bad decision* versus *is a bad kid* when parenting a child. A statement such as "You are a great kid, but you did not make a great decision today" puts the emphasis on a choice versus a shame-inducing statement, such as "I am so disappointed in you," which places blame on the child. It is important to make sure that you are not using shame-inducing statements when parenting any child, but especially when you have a child with sensory-based issues, because your child cannot help the way they feel. Children with difficulty regulating their nervous systems are often particularly sensitive to criticism and even more vulnerable to internalizing negative comments and statements. It is helpful to keep the focus on choices and consequences, rather than worthiness. Here is an example of a conversation between a parent and child named Pearson after an incident at a birthday party in which Pearson had a meltdown and had to be taken out of the party by his mom:

Mom: What happened yesterday at the party? You were so upset, and I did not know how to help you.

Pearson: I was disgusted by the sticky feeling on my fingers from eating the cake, and I lost it. I just could not stand the way my fingers felt, and I had to get out of there. I felt really sad afterward, like I was a really bad person.

Mom: Honey, I tried to get you to wash your hands, and you chose not to. Do you think that might have helped?

Pearson: Well, I could have washed my hands, but I really do not like the bathroom at that kid's house. It has a really funky smell in it, and I don't like going in there.

Mom: Okay, so are there other options for washing your hands there? How could you have made a different choice?

Pearson: I guess I could have done it in the kitchen or used a wet wipe. They had wet wipes at the party. I'm sorry. I know I was bad yesterday. I feel terrible because I missed all of the fun.

Mom: So you made a choice that did not work for you, but that's not being bad. Now you know that the next time something like this happens, you have the ability to make a different choice. Pearson, you responded when your nervous system was telling you that you were in danger, but you were really just uncomfortable. And the truth is that I could have made a different choice as well. I could have helped you problem solve how to get the stickiness off of your hands instead of just telling you to wash them. I am sorry for the choice that I made too. Maybe we can both work on making different choices in the future.

Moving Toward Success

No matter what age your child is, when you are dealing with regulation of the sensory nervous system, you are a big part of helping your child understand their body and behavior and change how they manage their sensory nervous system. As we have illustrated in this chapter, change is a process that might look a little different at different stages of your child's development. Also remember that sensory issues tend to get better with age for many children because their brains get better at integrating all of the sensory input that they are bombarded with in life. While a child may be extremely over-responsive at age six, they may be only mildly responsive at fifteen, even without any intervention at all. With your help and support, your child can learn new behaviors to become a better sensory regulator to the point that they will be able to manage their reactions independently as they age. Daily practice is important in establishing new neural pathways in the brain—for both of you. Each day you and your child can practice new responses and new behaviors that, over time, will become your normal responses. All of this is part of the journey called parenting.

Conclusion

This chapter has outlined your role as supporter and cheerleader at every stage of child development. We described how to support your child and how not to accommodate anxious reactions to sensory stimuli, while at the same time not punishing responses that your child does not yet know how to manage. We reviewed your role as a parent at various stages of child development, with your involvement decreasing as your child ages and becomes a better sensory regulator. We reviewed ways to focus on maintaining a healthy relationship with your child and how to keep the focus on behaviors that are positive and appropriate, rather than on negative or problematic behaviors. We also discussed ways to increase empathy for your child and focus on choices rather than judging them as a person, thus reducing shame. Your relationship with your child will begin to heal and grow through this process. At any age, when you are appropriately and actively involved in supporting your child and their sensory nervous system, the result is better coping, improved family functioning, and life-long positive change.

CHAPTER 9

Positive Self-Care for Parents

It is nearly impossible to be a good parent if you are stressed out and exhausted. Stress makes us vulnerable to poor decision making and doing things that we may regret later. Almost all parents will admit that they have had their fair share of bad moments as a parent, when they said or did things that they later regretted. However, it does no good to look back and remember the bad parenting moments. What does make sense is to focus on the present and the future, to make a plan for how you can be a more effective parent, one who is strong and less vulnerable to reacting in ways that are later regretted.

How do you do this? How do you reduce your stress and the probability of making bad decisions or engaging in reactive parenting in the future? This chapter is focused on helping you slow down and take a good look at your life, perhaps eliminating the things that are causing stress or at least altering them to limit their impact on you. For many parents, the notion of better self-care will sound odd. Often the first reaction is: "I don't have time." Sometimes people judge parents who spend time each week taking care of their health and well-being as selfish or even as bad parents. If you are reading this section and having an immediate negative reaction to the idea of self-care either because it takes time away from your child or children or because it sounds selfish, we ask that you allow yourself to be open to the idea of taking better care of yourself.

Here are some things to consider when making the decision to devote time to yourself. Think of this list as the things that you will gain by spending time each week engaged in self-care activities:

- improved problem solving

- increased ability to slow down and think before responding

- increased self-confidence

- improved happiness

- increased ability to manage your feelings

- improved ability to present a positive role model for your child

Spend some time and think about these important points. Do any of these resonate with you and your goals? If so, read on, and we will explore many different aspects of positive self-care. All of these changes will provide you with new skills and abilities to cope better with the challenges of parenting a sensory-sensitive child. Let's begin by evaluating sleep habits and routines.

Good Sleep

It is common for parents to go through periods in which they get less-than-adequate sleep, especially when they have young children in the house. How is your sleep? Do you get six to eight hours of sleep a night? Do you feel rested in the morning when you wake up?

Take a Moment: Begin to keep a journal of your evening behaviors and your sleep. Write down each night some details about your day: what you ate for dinner, whether or not you exercised, the amount of caffeine you ingested after three in the afternoon, what your stress level was for that day, and what activities you did just before going to bed. Start to notice whether certain behaviors impact your sleep. Do you notice that drinking a cup of coffee at seven at night affects your ability to fall asleep that night? Does screen time just before bed stimulate your brain, making it hard to fall asleep? Do you sleep differently on nights after you participated in vigorous exercise during the day? Note what things affect your sleep and begin to systematically change them so that your sleep is less impacted. The following is a list of things that are known to affect sleep in a negative way:

- caffeine

- alcohol

- screen time just before bed

- sedentary lifestyle (lack of exercise)

- napping during the day

- eating sugar close to bedtime

- eating too close to bedtime

- having a very different schedule from day to day

Conversely, the following things are known to affect sleep in a positive way:

- limiting caffeine intake after two in the afternoon

- limiting alcohol intake

- reading a book before bed (a print book, not an e-book)

- not using screens for an hour before sleep

- exercise regularly

- getting up at the same time each day and avoiding naps during the day

- avoiding sugar close to bedtime

- allowing three hours between eating and bedtime

- having the same bedtime ritual each night; doing your routine in the same way each night to train your body to get ready for sleep

- practicing relaxation, deep breathing, or meditation just before trying to fall asleep

For the next few weeks, try changing how you approach sleep. Change one thing at a time and make notes about what you noticed. Maybe reduce caffeine in the afternoons for three days and see how it affects your sleep. Next, increase your exercise and notice whether there is a difference in your ability to get restful sleep. Be kind to yourself and don't set unreasonable goals—this is all about your feeling better about yourself, not worse.

Always change one thing at a time so you will know which one is helping you sleep better. Keep the strategies that helped and let the others go.

Social Support

Social support simply refers to the people you have in your life who are there for you when you are in need. Social support can refer to a spouse, a family member (sister, brother, parent, cousin), a friend, a religious advisor or group, or a social group (exercise group, book club, school PTA). Do you have support when times get tough? Social support can really carry us through hard times, especially with our children. Finding other parents who have similar issues with their child can be incredibly validating and helpful in that it makes us feel less alone in our struggles. Sometimes this is not possible—and that is okay too. Other people can listen and support you, even if they cannot relate to your experiences. Bottom line: it is important to be able to spend time with others, talk about different topics, and enjoy activities in the company of other people. Spending time with people can be fun, takes your mind off of life stressors, allows you to give and receive support, and is a good distraction from daily obligations.

If you are feeling a lack of social support, think about ways that you could add people into your life. Are there groups that you have thought about joining where you could meet people who are like-minded? Are there friends you have lost touch with whom you could reach out to for support or to reconnect? Sometimes just connecting with one person can consequently connect you to countless others. If you find yourself resisting the idea of seeking social support, ask yourself why. What stops you from seeking the company of others? Is it possible that you want to be with others, but you have ideas or beliefs that hold you back? Sometimes we hold beliefs that are not true at all (such as *no one wants to be around me*, *people don't like me*, or *I don't have time to socialize*). If this is the case, take a moment to challenge these ideas. The best way to challenge a belief is to do the thing that you have been avoiding and see whether the belief is true. Maybe attend a social gathering that you might have avoided in the past and see what happens. It is possible that the assumptions and beliefs that you had about attending the gathering were wrong, that it was better than you had imagined. The only way you will ever know is to try.

Exercise

Exercise is one habit that can be a game changer for people undergoing stress. You may think that exercise is not possible with a child or children, but many people have found ways to add it to their lives successfully by choosing exercise that either involves their children (using exercise joggers for walking or jogging) or supports their presence (gyms with babysitting services). Sometimes exercise programs such as yoga or stretching can be found online on platforms such as YouTube and can be done at home, thus reducing the need to find a gym or buy a jogger. Some parents have made agreements with friends or neighbors to take turns watching each other's children so that the other can get in a workout.

Start by setting reasonable expectations for yourself. If you are currently not exercising at all, you may want to begin with a walk around your block or in your neighborhood. If you would like to increase your current exercise routine, consider adding one more session of activity. Increasing exercise should be done in increments. Sometimes people create unreasonable expectations for themselves and are not able to achieve them. This can feel like a failure. You may have to be creative, but it can be done. Know that taking care of your body not only reduces your stress level on a daily basis but also models good behavior for your child.

Take a Moment: Make a list of all of the different forms of exercise that you used to like to do—maybe a sport you played in school or an activity you did at camp. Maybe it was simply taking a walk in the park or swimming in a lake. Now make a list of different forms of exercise that you have wanted to try but never got around to it. Maybe you always wanted to try karate or kickboxing or wanted to learn to do yoga. Now, check off the ones that you think you would like to put into your life—things that you could research in the next week and see about adding in your life. In addition to the ones that you want to try in the near future, also make a list of exercises that you want to do but maybe will have to wait for later, when your children are in a different stage (like once they start elementary school). Perhaps you always wanted to join a tennis team, but it does not make sense until your children are school-aged and busy during the day. Commit to putting three different forms of exercise into your life in the next month to see what you like. Once you have tried three, choose the ones you want to continue to do.

Enjoyable Activities

Believe it or not, engaging in activities that you enjoy reduces your stress level. You may think that because you have a child or children, you do not have the time or energy to do things that you enjoy. This is a common trap that parents find themselves in. Becoming healthy means finding time to do things that make you happy and that are meaningful to you. How do we expect to enjoy life if we are not doing things that we enjoy? Whether you choose a creative activity such as painting, photography, writing, or knitting or something outdoors such as fishing, golfing, or going to a boat show, make sure that you are incorporating pleasurable activities into your life. Again, modeling good self-care for your child will be a gift to them. It teaches them to do the same: to do things that they enjoy and to develop healthy self-care habits for their lifetime.

Take a Moment: Make a list of twenty things that you enjoy doing. Perhaps you like to go to the movies, read a book, or try a new recipe. It does not need to be peak experiences, like traveling to Europe—just everyday things that you know you like to do. Once you have your list, circle the ones that you have done in the past week. Next, circle the ones you have done in the past month. Finally, circle the ones you have done in the past year. Hopefully, you will have circled almost everything on your list. Regardless, make a point to put these pleasurable activities into your routine each week. When we feel like we are only doing things for others and never doing anything that we enjoy (which can happen pretty easily when parenting), we can become resentful and angry. Make sure that you are doing things for you too!

Be Kind to Yourself

It is easy to be harsh and critical of ourselves. Judging ourselves can almost be second nature to some of us. Think about the voice in your head that talks to you all day long. If you actually met a real person on the street who said those things to you, how would you feel about that person? Would you like that person? Would you want to hang out with that person? The answer is often, "No, that person would be hard to spend time with." If this is the case for you, consider what kinds of things that inner voice says to you. Is the voice discouraging, judgmental, or negative? If you find that you feel supported and validated by the internal voice, that is fantastic! Sounds like you have a good sense of self-compassion and that your thoughts are likely encouraging, complimentary, and supportive.

However, many people experience an internal voice that is critical, making judgments all day long. Some voices are very harsh, saying things like *Why did you do that? You're so stupid! You should not have eaten that! You always say odd things. People think you are weird!* Certainly, you would not want to be friends with that person, would you? Imagine how it would be if you never said anything to yourself that you would not say to your best friend. Imagine how your thoughts and feelings would be different. Imagine what it would be like to feel supported and loved by this voice. How would that change your life?

Take a Moment: For five days, keep a journal of your thoughts, the things you say to yourself every day. You don't have to show anybody this journal. Maybe keep it on your phone in your notes app. Each day, review what you have written. Are you surprised at any of your thoughts? Are they more or less critical than you thought they would be? After the five days are up, go back and change the thoughts from the past five days to things that you would say to your best friend if they were in that situation. How would you treat your best friend differently? Now, for the next two weeks, practice using these best-friend thoughts instead of the old, critical thoughts. Notice how you feel differently with this kind of self-talk. Notice whether the kind words begin to come more naturally.

Disengage from the Battle! Practice Noticing—Not Judging—Your Child's Behavior

As parents, we get into habits of responding to our children. We respond almost without thinking, because we deal with their behavior day in and day out. Try not engaging in negative battles—when your child acts up, try just noticing what they are doing and comment without judging them. For example, if your son adamantly refuses to eat his dinner, even though this is what is on his hierarchy of best meals and he has his coping tools available to him, try responding like this:

Son: I am not eating my chicken. It's gross!

Parent: I know this is really hard for you and that you do not want to eat the chicken.

Son: You can't make me eat it!

Parent: You are right, and I will never make you eat anything. You can choose to eat it and to use your skills as we discussed, or you can choose not to.

Son: I am choosing not to! It's so gross!

Parent: I am sorry that you are making that choice. We are having toast with peanut butter and fruit for breakfast. Why don't you go wash up and get ready for bed.

Son: What? No dinner? I'm hungry! I want mac and cheese for dinner.

Parent: I am sorry that you chose not to follow the plan of using your new skills, but you can wait until we have breakfast in the morning if you choose not to use your skills and eat the chicken. [Parent leaves the room.]

Sometimes it is just not worth the argument, and it is best to walk away with the limit having been set. By not engaging, you take much of the energy out of the situation and stop a conflict from developing. Think about it like a game of tug-of-war. How do you win a game of tug-of-war? Many people respond that you tug harder and harder until you win, but there is another, more effective way to win. The way to win that we are suggesting is to let go, to allow the other person to fall back and you remain standing, in a place of control. Having a tug-of-war with your child only leads to a back-and-forth struggle; winning involves letting go. It takes two to have a conflict, and by letting go—that is, removing yourself or refusing to engage in the conflict—you can deescalate a battle with very little effort. Reacting in a different way also disarms the child; they are used to your old ways of responding and will push you to give that old response. Hold steady and do not go back to old ways, as that would keep the old habits in place.

Be Positive in the Face of Conflict

It is one thing to not respond in negative situations, as stated above, but it is another to practice remaining positive in the face of conflict. When your child is throwing metaphorical rocks, respond with throwing feathers. When your child says, "I hate you," respond with "I love you." When your child says, "You hate me," respond with "I love you, that is why I am helping you face this difficult thing, because I want you to be strong and be able to do this in the future."

Take a Moment: Make a list of all of the amazing things about your child—their sense of humor, intelligence, sense of style, ability to remember facts, and so on. Now, make a point to notice these things each day and to comment on them when you notice them. Even in the face of conflict, you can notice the positive aspects of your child. For example, in the scene above where the child did not want to eat his chicken, a parent might comment, "You are so strong-willed. That will serve you well in life." It is all too easy to fall into negative habits and begin "instructing" our children about how they "should" be. Staying positive, even in the face of conflict, helps us support our children in all situations, no matter how frustrating. Remember, this work is hard for your child, and they are simply telling you through their behavior that they are working hard to regulate their system.

Stay in the Present

Usually when we get sucked into conflict or battles, it is because we are not aware of what is going on, and we react out of habit or mindlessly. Being mindful means that you are aware of yourself in the present moment; you can see what is happening and can react with intention, not with intensity. Being mindful means that you are not distracted by the multitude of things going on around you and that you have the presence of mind to regulate your responses. Mindfulness is all about noticing what you are experiencing, without judging it or reacting to the experience thoughtlessly. If you are hungry, you might notice your hunger and notice where in your body you feel the sensation of hunger—you might even think about what foods would nourish your body—without doing anything at all. After becoming aware of your internal sensations, you might then decide whether eating is the right thing to do in that moment (maybe dinner will be ready in thirty minutes, and it makes more sense to wait), and make a plan for when and what to eat. Being aware of our moment-to-moment experience, without judging it, is the key to staying happy, calm, and less anxious.

Now think about how you might apply this skill to interactions with your child. When your child is over-responding to an experience, you might say, "I see this is getting really hard for you," or "This seems to bother you. Let's think of something together that might help." These examples demonstrate a parent who is staying in the moment, not reacting with frustration or judgment. Keeping your cool will help de-escalate the situation, and it allows your child to feel heard and understood. So not only do you stay calm, but it helps your child too!

Take a Moment: A simple mindfulness exercise that can be practiced each day is something that we call "thought watching." Sit quietly and comfortably in a place where you will not be disturbed, without any phones or other things that ring. Close your eyes and simply notice your breathing. Notice the breath going in and out of your nose. Try to stay with your breath and just notice what it feels like to breathe. Because you are human and alive, you will notice your thoughts begin to wander. Like a puppy, your thoughts will wander away from the breath and onto other things. When you realize that your thoughts have wandered, notice where they wander to and gently return them to the breath. Be careful not to judge yourself for having thoughts that wander; it is normal, and we all do this. Just return the thoughts to the breath while making a note of what brain habits you have: where do your thoughts tend to go? Many people report that their thoughts wander to the laundry list of things they need to do later in the day (planning) or things that they wish they had done differently in the past (regretting), or maybe they wander to self-criticism (self-judgment), or maybe they move to fearing some dismal outcome in the future that is not guaranteed (often called "catastrophizing"). No matter where your thoughts go, keep returning them to the breath, but notice where they went.

Do this exercise every day for five to ten minutes and, after three to four weeks, you will begin to notice that you are better able to stay focused on the breath for longer periods of time. You will also begin to recognize the thought habits that you have, both while doing this practice and while moving around in your life. For example, you might be driving to pick up your child from school and notice your thoughts wandering to "planning." Once you notice this thought habit, you can start to focus on the breath, which returns your focus to the present moment, allowing you to be fully present when you pick up your child. Practicing thought watching is just one way to work toward mindfulness and improve your ability to cope with stress and react with intention. With practice, people who are more mindful are better able to see their habits and notice their thoughts or impulses before acting. Noticing this allows you time to think about what the best response might be, one that might be different from your typical habit.

Keep a Daily Schedule for the Family

Believe it or not, one thing that helps parents and children stay calm and feel good is to have a schedule. If you or your children (or all of you) do not like to have a schedule, this is a sign that you probably need one! Schedules make the day predictable, help children feel safe, and promote a sense of routine and family norms. Having a schedule also helps reduce having to deal with random requests—such as "Can we go to the toy store?"—when going to the toy store on a Wednesday afternoon is *never* on the schedule. Schedules take a bit of effort to create, but they are a game changer for families with children who have issues with sensory regulation.

Take a Moment: In your journal, create a separate blank sheet for each day of the week. Now, write down the things that happen on an ongoing basis, like school, after-school activities, and work obligations. Next, write down wake-up times and bedtimes, chores, homework times, as well as times for meals and meal preparation. Then add in times for self-care for you and playtime for your child. See what times are left open. Any long stretch of open time can be designated for hobbies, enjoyable activities, and other things that you have wanted to add in to your schedule. Weekends may look a bit different than weekdays, but make a schedule for weekends as well. What you will have at the end of this exercise is a skeleton schedule for your family. Each week you can add in or delete activities as things change, but overall, your basic schedule should stay relatively consistent over time.

Believe it or not, families who work on a schedule have less conflict and less drama than families who do not. If you have not had a schedule in the past and are trying to institute one, know that there will likely be a period of transition—and possible pushback from your family members. Give it one to three months for everyone to settle in to the schedule and get used to the new routine.

Conclusion

In earlier chapters, we explored different ways that you can improve your interactions with your child by describing and noticing behavior rather than judging, by being positive during a conflict, and by staying in the present with your child. In order to truly embrace these skills, it is important to develop positive self-care practices. These can include getting better sleep, increasing daily exercise, spending more time doing enjoyable activities, and spending time with friends. In addition, paying close attention to how you talk to yourself and creating a positive, best-friend type of internal dialogue can be extremely helpful. Practicing being mindful will give you the ability to be present for your child and reduce unwanted, reactive responses. Finally, creating a predictable and routine schedule helps the family develop a rhythm that creates a sense of safety and security for all members.

The benefits of spending time focusing your own needs will be far-reaching, benefiting both you and your child. The skills discussed in this chapter will help you build the necessary, internal resources to cope when your child is having a difficult time and displaying challenging behaviors. You will also provide a positive example for your child, teaching them to take good care of themselves and to be positive, proactive, and intentional. Devoting time to positive self-care and healthy habits is important at all ages and stages of life! Next, in our final chapter, we will turn our attention to the family as whole.

CHAPTER 10

The Bigger Picture
Where Do We Go from Here?

Where We Have Been

The Nervous System

In the previous chapters you have learned more than you ever thought you would about the nervous system and how it works. Our unique nervous system helps us interact with the world and can impact our preferences, emotions, learning, and behavior. You learned about the sympathetic and parasympathetic systems and how they control arousal and calming. This balance of arousal and calming helps a person maintain a sense of equilibrium and homeostasis. If a person feels too aroused, they might seek calm, while if a person feels too calm or even bored, they might seek arousal.

You also learned about the different parts of the sensory nervous system. The far senses include vision, hearing, smell, touch, and taste, while the near senses include interoceptive (heart rate, digestion, breathing), proprioceptive (body position and space), and vestibular (sensing movement). All of the senses give a person information about the outside and inside world so that they can adjust their behavior, if needed, to achieve a sense of comfort. For example, if a person senses hunger (near senses) and cold (far senses), they can seek food and warmth. In addition to comfort, another important function that the nervous system performs is that of keeping the body safe from harm. If the nervous system senses danger, the sympathetic nervous system (arousal) is activated and readies the body to fight, flee, or freeze, all of which can rescue the body from harm. In a regulated nervous system, all of these functions work together to keep the body feeling balanced, safe, and functioning well. But, as you have learned, not everyone has a regulated nervous system.

Problems with Regulation

When the nervous system has difficulties with the intake, interpretation, or processing of sensory information, this is reflected in emotions and behavior. As you learned, if I feel cold much of the time, I will carry a sweater with me and might wear long sleeves in 65-degree weather, while another person might experience 65 degrees as the perfect temperature for shorts and a T-shirt. Neither is right, and neither is wrong—they are just different. In other words, our unique sensory systems impact our lives in a multitude of ways. Using this example, one might say that my nervous system is over-responsive to touch and sensing temperature, while the other person may be under-responsive to this same sense. In more extreme cases, where the senses are very heightened or very dulled, we see more extreme emotional and behavioral reactions to sensory triggers that can be quite unusual and difficult to understand to the untrained eye.

We walked you through the different experiences of both over- and under-responsive children regarding the various senses of the nervous system, particularly when responses are more extreme. We explained what behaviors typically occur when each of the senses is either over- or under-responsive. We explained how these over- or under-responses can mimic the symptoms of various common, childhood psychiatric disorders (obsessive-compulsive disorder, oppositional defiant disorder, generalized anxiety disorder, social anxiety, and panic disorder) or oftentimes co-occur with certain childhood disorders such as attention deficit hyperactivity disorder, persistent tic disorders, body-focused repetitive behaviors, and autism spectrum disorders. In the first half of this book, we hope that we effectively illustrated how pervasive the sensory nervous system can be in impacting a child's learning and behavior. Understanding your child's unique nervous system helps you understand why they behave the way they do, and it gives you clues to what you can do to help them.

The Road to Regulation

The second half of this book was spent describing how to help your child successfully regulate their nervous system. Understanding your child's nervous system is important, but knowing how to teach them the skills to improve their sensory regulation is the key to success. We walked you through the formula for success in developing a tolerance for sensory triggers:

Experience + Sensory Soothing + Coping Skills + Making It Fun
= Tolerance for the Sensory Triggers

We took a step-by-step approach in teaching you how to build an Experience Ladder for each of your child's sensory triggers. We reviewed the various coping skills your child will need to help them be able to face the challenging sensory triggers and to ultimately tolerate uncomfortable sensory triggers that were previously difficult to manage. We described how this approach looks for specific behaviors that are the result of over- and under-responsive nervous systems. We reviewed how to develop empathy for your child, how to stay positive, and how to use reward systems and encouragement—and how not to use punishment or accommodation—to improve your child's behavior. We reviewed self-care and how you can help yourself before helping your child, so that you can be a better parent to your child. Now, where do we go from here? How do you put all of this together to forge a path of support, empathy, and teamwork so your child can move into the future with a sense of control and confidence in their ability to regulate their nervous system?

Think about this journey of parenting as just that—a journey. As parents, we are constantly learning and adjusting to our child's needs, developmental stages, and the life challenges that present themselves. We must all be willing to use what we have learned to adapt and change as we go through the process of parenting.

Let's look at Molly and her challenging behaviors around schoolwork. Molly loves to be neat (she says "perfect") and gets upset when things don't look just how she wants them to look. Let's see how her Molly and her mother worked as a team to create a workable plan to manage schoolwork in a healthy way.

Molly is a nine-year-old who has become increasing more uncomfortable with doing work in a space that has extra "things" in it. If there are pencils, pens, papers, paper clips, or any item that Molly feels does not belong, she gets upset and cries, refusing to do her work. It is hard for her to settle down to complete her homework after an "episode," as her parents call it, no matter how clean her space is. These episodes have been happening with more frequency at school as well, due to needing to have more school supplies on her desk during class to facilitate learning. Molly likes her schoolwork environment to be pristine. This is impractical, of course, because school desks often have supplies on them. Molly's mother spoke with her about her inability to work in a space that is not, in her mind, "perfect."

Mother:	Honey, I have noticed that you are getting more upset each time you sit down to do your homework.
Molly:	Yeah, that's because I can't find a place to work! There is nowhere in the house for me to do my homework.
Mother:	Well, the desk in the kitchen used to work for you. Why doesn't that work any longer?
Molly:	You have all your stuff on the desk. There is no place for me to put my paper.
Mother:	Let's look together. I see lots of space. Don't you?
Molly:	Well, there is a cup of pens and pencils. There is a notebook and a pile of papers on the desk. I can't work here!

Mother:	Yes, but there is also plenty of workspace to put your own papers and supplies.
Molly:	I don't want anything on the desk. It needs to be completely clean or else I can't concentrate.
Mother:	Honey, desks have supplies on them, even in school. It's important to learn how to work in a space that is "clean enough," since you will have to do this throughout your life. Remember how we have been working on challenging your nervous system? Let's create a plan to challenge this too. Let's start with a reward system. What would be fun to earn?
Molly:	I love baking cookies. Could I earn some really fun cookie cutters?
Mother:	That's a great idea. We could get some ingredients too. As soon as you earn the cookie cutters, you can bake a batch of cookies.
Molly:	That sounds fun.
Mother:	Now, let's talk about how to earn those cookie cutters. Remember the Experience Ladders we created with other things like hearing loud sounds and wearing socks? How about we make one for this challenge too.
Molly:	Okay. I don't like anything on the desk—so how about having one thing out on the desk that "doesn't belong"?
Mother:	All right. How about if that one thing is a small bowl of chocolate candies?
Molly:	Oh, I love that!
Mother:	What other skills worked for you in the past, when you worked on your other ladders?

Molly: I liked to use the deep breathing and calming thoughts. Maybe I could breathe deeply for three minutes before sitting down to do homework. I could also remember to tell myself "I can do this!" And I can remember the cookie cutters I want to earn!

Mother: Fantastic! How about I give you a point for every time you practice deep breathing and calming thoughts, and every time you are able to do your homework with the bowl of chocolate candies on the table? As we add other things to the desk, you can earn more points for those too.

Molly: Okay, I also remember that I liked when you turned on the lavender smell diffuser. Can we do that too?

Mother: Of course!

Molly: How many points do I need to earn to get the cookie cutters? Can we say five?

Mother: Well, I think you will get to five pretty quickly, so how about we say twenty, does that sounds good?

Molly: Sure!

Here you can see how Molly and her mother have discussed her behavior and agreed to a comprehensive plan. In order to help Molly get on board with the idea quickly, a reward system was agreed upon first. Next, Molly and her mother talked about some sensory-soothing items that have worked for her in the past. In addition, Molly decided to carry around a smooth stone as well as listen to classical music while she does her homework. These helped soothe her nervous system while she tolerated a workspace that had candies and other items in it. As an added bonus, when Molly completed her homework, she was allowed to eat the chocolates. This really made the challenge more fun, and she found that it was not as hard as she thought it was going to be.

Getting started is often one of the biggest hurdles. Having a factual, nonjudgmental discussion that encourages your child toward change and healthy behaviors is important, as Molly and her mother showed. Also, don't forget the reward system; it encourages your child to engage and motivates them to work hard.

Looking Forward

What Happens When Problems with Sensory Regulation Are Not Addressed?

What happens if you miss these issues or just let the problems with sensory regulation go—hoping they will resolve on their own? Well, for starters, not understanding the reason for your child's behavior can lead to confusion, frustration, and family conflict. In addition, children can develop unusual or inappropriate means of coping, as well as have an image of themselves that is negative and colored by feelings of shame. Children may lash out or blame others when they feel uncomfortable. Additionally, sometimes children may grow into adults who tend toward isolation and avoidance of people, places, and things that make them uncomfortable.

Intimacy Problems

Problems with sensory regulation in childhood can sometimes lead to problems with developing healthy relationships and connections to others in adulthood. It's hard to be close to someone when physically being touched has felt uncomfortable since earliest childhood. Likewise, when chewing, sniffing, or talking is distressing or even distracting to the listener, it's impossible to gain trust or get close to a person. Other times, those with challenges with sensory regulation blame others for their discomfort, not understanding that it is their nervous system that is the issue. A benign behavior, such as eating popcorn at a movie theater (creating rustling noises and chewing sounds) can cause a person who is auditory over-responsive to vehemently blame the popcorn eater for ruining the movie due to the terrible noise, causing a scene in the theater.

Finally, people who have sensory regulation issues that are not addressed in childhood may grow up believing that they are different, strange, or unlovable. Unaddressed sensory regulation can lead to lower self-esteem and a poor sense of self-efficacy. Teaching your child to manage their nervous system helps them feel confident and gives them the skills they need to manage intimacy in the future. As we learned earlier, children with poor sensory regulation tend to be rigid. Having a rigid approach to life in childhood, if not addressed, leads to a rigid approach to life as an adult. Remember how we talked about raw spaghetti versus cooked spaghetti? We want to teach our children to behave like cooked spaghetti, to be flexible and not break when things do not go their way. An important part of success in life is the ability to be flexible and to adapt to new situations. If a person is not adaptable to the inevitable changes of life, they will likely struggle with intimate relationships and other important aspects of functioning in adult life.

Family Discord

Similarly, challenges with sensory processing almost always affect family functioning. The family member with processing difficulties can be particularly angry at others for causing them discomfort by putting items in the wrong place, cooking food that has an unpleasant smell, chewing too loudly, or trying to hug them. Left unchecked, these feelings can grow and cause rifts in the family, oftentimes making the poor regulator the scapegoat for family tension. Conflict within the family may also lead to less family time, fewer family vacations, and particularly stressful holidays. However, this does not have to be the case. Children with sensory regulation issues have many strengths. Helping your child learn how to manage their nervous system and emphasize their natural abilities, while teaching them to cope with their challenges, is a recipe for success in life! Let's look at some significant positive characteristics of people with poor sensory regulation.

The Positive Side of Doing This Work

Being Emotionally Sensitive

As we have seen, being sensitive from a sensory standpoint can lead to behavioral overreactions and meltdowns. Once children learn about their sensitivities and learn to cope with them and thrive, they are able to function well in life. In addition, sensory-dysregulated individuals possess the ability to be truly emotionally sensitive as well. Being emotionally sensitive allows these children to be empathetic and caring toward others, if these qualities are encouraged. Children growing up with over- or under-responsive systems understand what discomfort feels like and can be extremely kind toward others who may be suffering. This translates to having excellent qualities as a friend. These children can be loving, stable partners who are reliable, understanding, and good listeners. These are the children whom others may turn to when they have problems or are feeling sad. Being a good, nonjudgmental listener is an important and sought-after quality in a friend and partner.

You want to encourage this quality in your child. If you have found yourself telling your child "you are too sensitive," make an effort to change this statement. Telling a child that they are too sensitive is judgmental and is a criticism that is not helpful. The last thing you want to do is encourage your child to be less sensitive! Maybe a more accurate statement would be "you are having trouble managing this trigger—let's see how we can help you use your coping skills." Being sensitive is good and should be celebrated! We would like to emphasize the benefits of being sensitive and how this very characteristic may enhance their relationships in the future. We want to help them be children who grow into sensitive, productive adults who tend to be stable, reliable employees and who are trusted by their peers.

Being Artistic

Children with sensory regulation issues can also be extremely creative. Having over- or under-responsive visual, tactile, and auditory systems lends itself to talent in the areas of painting, photography, graphic design, fashion design, interior design, architecture, engineering, sculpture, and music, to name a few. These skills require a sharp attention to visual, tactile, and auditory detail. Many successful artists and musicians grew up with sensory regulation challenges. It is possible that what looks like a problem in childhood can turn into a career path in adulthood. This is why it is so important to encourage your child to explore their nervous system and not judge themselves for their regulation issues. We hope that this book has been a good platform to teach both you and your child how to see sensory differences as normal and to embrace them and cope with them, rather than judge them and feel shameful for them. Who knows—it may be that the very things that bother your child early on are the things that will assist them in the future!

Being a Creative Problem Solver

Many people who experience sensory regulation challenges are extremely creative, are good at thinking outside the box, and are excellent at problem solving. These people are invaluable as team members when working on challenging projects. They can often find really interesting, clever solutions to stubborn problems. Think about what you and your child have learned throughout this book: you have hopefully learned ways to approach difficult situations from another perspective, with love and support, and without judgment. The nature of these interventions is creative and out of the box. Learning that wearing headphones with your favorite music, smelling eucalyptus, and telling yourself kind words while eating in the loud, stinky school cafeteria is a creative approach to a seemingly unsolvable problem. Your child is learning that no problem is unsolvable, that interventions are creative, and that there are no wrong ways to feel! Learning acceptance of their sensory functioning is an essential skill taught throughout this book and will translate into acceptance of other unpleasant events in the future. Having learned these skills, your child will be more effective at targeting creative solutions to problems, rather than resisting the problem itself. Through this work, you are helping your child become a more resilient person in the future.

Conclusion

We hope that through reading this book you have gained a clearer understanding of your child, their behavior, and ways to help them regulate their unique nervous system. As you have seen and have likely experienced firsthand, there are many complicated emotions and behaviors that result from having sensory regulation difficulties. These emotions and behaviors often affect the child, the family, the school environment, and relationships with their peers. Children can display unusual soothing practices, abrupt meltdowns, and quirky behaviors; they can lash out and shut down. Over time, these behaviors can create social challenges, impact family harmony, lead to emotional dysregulation, and create problems with self-concept and self-confidence.

Fortunately, there is a path to healthy behaviors using the formula described throughout this book. First, become aware of the various sensory triggers that cause discomfort for your child. Second, create an Experience Ladder to help your child move closer to the sensory trigger with comfort and confidence. Third, find many diverse sensory-soothing items to use during the experience to make it more tolerable. Fourth, find some helpful statements that your child can use when facing the difficult sensory trigger. Finally, make it fun and encouraging for you and your child!

Most importantly, we want you to create a home environment that is filled with empathy, support, and patience. Taking care of yourself along the way helps you remain just that—empathic, supportive, and patient! Having a predictable routine also helps the entire family function better and feel a sense of security within the home.

Remember that there are plenty of positive aspects of having sensory regulation issues, especially if you help your child learn to manage them successfully, as outlined in this chapter. Your child is likely to be empathic, artistic, and a creative problem solver as a result of dealing with these challenges. Remember, our character is built from our struggles, not from our achievements. Watching your child struggle is hard, but supporting them through the struggles, loving them unconditionally, and teaching them ways to manage their over- or under-responsive nervous system allows them to develop a foundation of resilience and fortitude that will help them throughout their life.

References

Ayres, A. J. 1966. "Interrelations Among Perceptual-Motor Abilities in a Group of Normal Children." *American Journal of Occupational Therapy* 20: 288–292.

Ayres, A. J. 1972. "Some General Principles of Brain Function." In *Sensory Integration and Learning Disorders*, edited by A. J. Ayres. Los Angeles: Western Psychological Services.

Golomb, R. G., and S. Mouton-Odum. 2016. *Psychological Interventions for Children with Sensory Dysregulation*. New York: Guilford Press.

Kranowitz, C. S. 2005. *The Out-of-Sync Child: Recognizing and Coping with Sensory Processing Disorder*. New York: Penguin.

Suzanne Mouton-Odum, PhD, is a licensed psychologist and expert in treating children with anxiety disorders, behavioral disorders, and sensory-based issues since 1995. She holds faculty positions at both Baylor College of Medicine, and the University of Houston. She is author of four other books, and director of Psychology Houston, PC in Houston, TX.

Ruth Goldfinger Golomb, LCPC, is a senior clinician, supervisor, and codirector of the training program at the Behavior Therapy Center of Greater Washington, where she has worked for more than thirty years. She specializes in the treatment of anxiety disorders in children and adults, and has conducted numerous trainings, workshops, and seminars on these topics.

Foreword writer Fred Penzel, PhD, is a licensed psychologist, and executive director of Western Suffolk Psychological Services. He specializes in the cognitive/behavioral treatment of obsessive-compulsive disorder (OCD), phobias, post-traumatic stress disorder (PTSD), and more.

Real change *is* possible

For more than forty-five years, New Harbinger has published proven-effective self-help books and pioneering workbooks to help readers of all ages and backgrounds improve mental health and well-being, and achieve lasting personal growth. In addition, our spirituality books offer profound guidance for deepening awareness and cultivating healing, self-discovery, and fulfillment.

Founded by psychologist Matthew McKay and Patrick Fanning, New Harbinger is proud to be an independent, employee-owned company. Our books reflect our core values of integrity, innovation, commitment, sustainability, compassion, and trust. Written by leaders in the field and recommended by therapists worldwide, New Harbinger books are practical, accessible, and provide real tools for real change.

 **newharbinger**publications

MORE BOOKS from
NEW HARBINGER PUBLICATIONS

**HELPING YOUR CHILD
WITH EXTREME
PICKY EATING**

A Step-by-Step Guide for
Overcoming Selective Eating,
Food Aversion &
Feeding Disorders

978-1626251106 / US $17.95

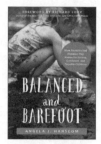

BALANCED & BAREFOOT

How Unrestricted Outdoor
Play Makes for Strong,
Confident & Capable Children

978-1626253735 / US $17.95

**HELPING YOUR
ANXIOUS CHILD,
SECOND EDITION**

A Step-by-Step Guide
for Parents

978-1572245754 / US $18.95

**HELPING YOUR CHILD
WITH LANGUAGE-BASED
LEARNING DISABILITIES**

Strategies to Succeed in School
& Life with Dyslexia,
Dysgraphia, Dyscalculia, ADHD
& Processing Disorders

978-168400989 / US $17.95

**PARENTING A CHILD
WHO HAS INTENSE
EMOTIONS**

Dialectical Behavior Therapy
Skills to Help Your Child
Regulate Emotional Outbursts
& Aggressive Behaviors

978-1572246492 / US $19.95

**ANXIETY RELIEF
FOR KIDS**

On-the-Spot Strategies to
Help Your Child Overcome
Worry, Panic & Avoidance

978-1626259539 / US $16.95

newharbingerpublications
1-800-748-6273 / newharbinger.com

(VISA, MC, AMEX / prices subject to change without notice)
Follow Us

Don't miss out on new books in the subjects that interest you.
Sign up for our **Book Alerts** at **newharbinger.com/bookalerts**

Register your **new harbinger** titles for additional benefits!

When you register your **new harbinger** title—purchased in any format, from any source—you get access to benefits like the following:

- Downloadable accessories like printable worksheets and extra content

- Instructional videos and audio files

- Information about updates, corrections, and new editions

Not every title has accessories, but we're adding new material all the time.

Access free accessories in 3 easy steps:

1. Sign in at NewHarbinger.com (or **register** to create an account).

2. Click on **register a book**. Search for your title and click the **register** button when it appears.

3. Click on the **book cover or title** to go to its details page. Click on **accessories** to view and access files.

That's all there is to it!

If you need help, visit:

NewHarbinger.com/accessories

new harbinger
CELEBRATING
40 YEARS